# L ITERATURE IN THE MODERN WORLD

# BLOCK 4 ———
# LITERATURE AND IDEOLOGY

*Prepared for the course team by Angus Calder, Roger Day, Cicely Palser Havely, Graham Martin, Dennis Walder and Keith Whitlock*

GW01417715

- School tie
- gender role and identity - (reversal of
- materialism (Swede - EK etc)

A 3 1 9

**Arts: a third level course**

The Open University

## The course team

Richard Allen (author)
Jenny Bardwell (BBC producer)
Richard Bessel (author)
Dinah Birch (author)
Angus Calder (author)
Kate Clements (editor)
Tony Coe (BBC series producer, author)
Charles Cooper (BBC producer)
Tony Coulson (Library)
Abigail Croydon (editor)
Roger Day (author)
Andrew Ferguson (course manager)
Margaret Harvey (block rapporteur)
Cicely Palser Havely (author)
Pam Higgins (graphic designer)
Barbara Humphreys (secretary)
G.D. Jayalakshimi (BBC producer)
Denis Johnson (tuition group chair)
Maggie Lawson (Project Control)
Beth Martin (BBC producer)

Graham Martin (course team chair, author)
Mags Noble (BBC producer)
W.R. Owens (editor of anthologies)
John Pettit (editor)
Michael Rossington (author)
Betty Talks (BBC producer)
Nora Tomlinson (tuition group)
Dennis Walder (author)
Keith Whitlock (author)
Amanda Willett (BBC producer)
Richard Wilson (block rapporteur)

### Consultants

Dr Pamela Morris, member of the Open University's teaching and counselling staff (block assessor)
Professor Michael Wood, department of English literature at the University of Exeter (external assessor)

The Open University
Walton Hall, Milton Keynes MK7 6AA

First published 1991. Reprinted 1995, 1996, 1998

Typeset in 10 on 12 point Palatino.

Printed in the United Kingdom by Page Bros, Norwich

ISBN 0 7492 1038 9

This block is part of an Open University course. The complete list of blocks is given at the end of this binding.

If you have not enrolled on the course and would like to buy this or other Open University material, please write to Open University Educational Enterprises Limited, 12 Cofferidge Close, Stony Stratford, Milton Keynes MK11 1BY, United Kingdom.

If you wish to enquire about enrolling as an Open University student, please write to: The Admissions Office, The Open University, PO Box 48, Walton Hall, Milton Keynes MK7 6AB, United Kingdom.

1.4

# Contents

(*Angus Calder wrote Section 5; Section 6 is by Roger Day; Sections 1, 2, 4 and 9 are by Cicely Palser Havely, Section 3 is by Graham Martin, Section 8 by Dennis Walder and Section 7 by Keith Whitlock. Richard Allen wrote the last part of Section 6*)

## Required reading

Rudyard Kipling, 'A Sahibs' War' (in the Prose Anthology)

Albert Camus (1983) *The Outsider*, trans. J. Laredo, Penguin (optional set book)

Muriel Spark (1965) *The Prime of Miss Jean Brodie*, Penguin (set book)

Flannery O'Connor, 'Revelation' (in the Prose Anthology)

Federico García Lorca, *Yerma* (in the Drama Anthology)

Athol Fugard, John Kani, Winston Ntshona, *The Island* (in the Drama Anthology)

*From the A319 Reader*

Terry Eagleton, 'Marxist criticism'

Pierre Macherey, 'The text says what it does not say'

Lionel Trilling, 'Freud and literature'

Etienne Balibar and Pierre Macherey, 'On literature as an ideological form'

Jean-Paul Sartre, 'Situation of the writer in 1947'

Theodor Adorno, 'Commitment'

(The A319 Reader is *Literature in the Modern World*, edited by Dennis Walder, 1990, Oxford University Press / The Open University.)

## Broadcasts/cassettes

TV6 *'The Island'* (linked to Section 8)

TV7 *In the Market Place* (Section 1)

Radio 6 *Literature and Ideology* (Section 1)

Radio 7 *F.G. Lorca's 'Yerma'* (Section 7)

Audio-cassette 2 Side 2, 'Extracts from *Yerma* by F.G. Lorca' (Section 7)

(See also the Broadcast and Cassette Notes.)

## Aims and objectives

The aims of this block are:

(a)  to help you be aware of the variety of ways in which an understanding of ideology is relevant to literary studies;

(b)  to debate the extent to which works of literature engage with politics;

(c)  to introduce some of the basic aims and tenets of Marxist criticism and to debate some of the differences between the materialist and essentialist positions;

(d)  to exercise some of these theoretical positions in relation to a variety of texts.

# 1  Literature and ideology

*1.1*  Section 1 is divided into two main parts:

(a)  definitions of ideology;

(b)  Marxism and ideology.

The first sets out some basic definitions and poses general questions. The second guides you through a chapter from Terry Eagleton's *Marxism and Literary Criticism*, which is in the A319 Reader. It is very important that you work through this material before proceeding to the case-studies in the rest of this block. Before continuing with this section, you should also revise Block 1 Section 4 and, even more important, Block 2 Section 8, 'Modernism and "ideology"'.

*1.2*  'Ideology' was discussed and defined in the foundation course A102; here are a few key explanations from the relevant units[1] :

*(i)  The 'dominant ideology' thesis*

> ...the groups which dominate in society try to maintain their dominance by making *their* values acceptable to subordinate groups, by a *systematic misrepresentation* of social relationships. In this way it is possible to maintain an unequal society in which those who are subordinate comply without needing to be threatened or coerced. The ideology by which their compliance is thus secured would be what is called a dominant ideology.
>
> (The Open University, 1986, p.73)

*(ii)  The Marxist usage*

> Ideology as Marx used the term, has the appearance of objective fact but its purpose is to serve the interests of one class over and against those of another.
>
> (Ibid., p.112)

*(iii)  Production, consumption and status*

> Pictures, poems, performances and periodicals are not only structures of meaning, although they are that; they are also, in an important sense, commodities, like plates, pills, pens, patterns – human products that coexist, which are made by and for people, and so are subject to the same ascertainable social and economic laws.
>
> (Ibid., p.11)

## Definitions of 'ideology'

### What is 'ideology'?

*1.3*  To many, I suspect, the word implies a forceful and unsubtle urging of oversimplified political argument, something quite at odds with the more agreeable complexities and uncertainties of literature. It is a term which you may associate more with sociology and politics than study of the arts, and it has been used in a variety of sometimes contradictory ways. The following definitions are taken from *The Penguin Dictionary of Sociology*:

[1]Students who have taken A102 might like to refer back to Units 20–21 pages 73–4 and 110–12, and Unit 22 pages 8–13.

One of the most debated concepts in sociology, ideology may be provisionally defined as beliefs, attitudes and opinions which form a set, whether tightly or loosely related. The term has been used in three important senses: (1) to refer to very specific kinds of belief; (2) to refer to beliefs that are in some sense distorted or false; (3) to refer to any set of beliefs, covering everything from scientific knowledge, to religion, to everyday beliefs about proper conduct, irrespective of whether it is true or false.

(Abercrombie, 1984)

It is a word with a complex history and a complex usage. Definition (1) is very simple: we speak of a Communist ideology or a Thatcherite ideology, an Islamic ideology or even a Green ideology, and know what we mean. Definition (2) reminds us that the word can have very definite, pejorative overtones. Indeed, both the 'conservative' Napoleon on the one hand, and Marx and Engels on the other, used the word pejoratively at times, and as Raymond Williams says, the former's usage is still common in conservative criticism of any social policy which is – in part or in whole – derived from social theory in a conscious way (Williams, 1983, p.126).

*1.4* For Marx and Engels, in *The German Ideology* (1845–47), ideology in one important sense was *false* thought: 'the illusion of [a] class about itself.' In this sense it overlaps with another important Marxist concept, 'false consciousness' – the idea that class interests blind us to the true nature of our actions, as Engels wrote in a letter to Franz Mehring (1893):

> Ideology is a process accomplished by the so-called thinker consciously indeed but with a false consciousness. The real motives remain unknown to him, otherwise it would not be an ideological process at all. Hence he imagines false or apparent motives.

Confusingly, however, the word in definition (3) – 'any set of beliefs' – has also been much used in the Marxist tradition with no sense of illusion or falsity. (Williams quotes Marx's *Contribution to the Critique of Political Philosophy*, 1859: 'the legal, political, religious, aesthetic or philosophic – in short ideological – forms.')

*1.5* At first sight definition (3) may seem too general to be useful. A Marxist might tighten it up a little by saying: 'any set of ideas which arise from a given set of material interests' (Williams, op. cit., p.129). Of course in practice there is an enormous variety of 'sets of material interests', not just those corresponding to the main class groups: an example suggested by Block 3 would be that of a male, English, Catholic, ex-army officer (like Waugh), who will have a different ideology from – say – a Scottish Presbyterian serving in the ranks of the Women's Royal Naval Service.

**What has ideology got to do with literature?**

*1.6* Some very simple things and some very complex ones:

First, some literary texts were deliberately written to promote a cause. If you studied A102 you will remember Charles Dickens's *Hard Times*. Another famous example from the nineteenth century is Harriet Beecher Stowe's anti-slavery novel *Uncle Tom's Cabin*. (*Pro*-slavery novels were written to refute it!) More recent examples include feminist novels of the 1960s and 70s such as Marilyn French's *The Women's Room*.

*1.7* However, works that promote a cause most simplistically are generally rather uninteresting and are not represented on this course. Empirically, it seems that literature is more 'interesting' to us the more complex its ideology. Those texts that, by general agreement, can be called 'literature' are seldom single-minded, not so much because the author intentionally ranges over different possibilities and points of view but because a text contains more than the author knows (sometimes to the extent that the overt message is contradicted by the hidden one) – a theme that will be developed in the case-studies. The texts in this block (and the whole course) are all 'interesting' cases, which do not reflect a simple ideological position, even where, with varying emphases, they may seem to be arguing a cause. But this empirical notion of what is interesting presupposes a great deal about the ideology of the *reader*. Someone from a totally different culture might find an airport novel, with its far from complex expression of Western secular values, very interesting.

1.8   Second, should literature take on causes, or rub shoulders with politics? You might want to say that it can do what it wants – how can there be any kind of proscription except that which is imposed by the limits of language? But you will remember from Block 2, in particular Sections 1 and 8, that the Modernists (partly because they were tired of the campaigning earnestness of the Victorians) declared that the condition to which their art should aspire was apolitical – resistant, in fact, to all ideologies. In practice this could not work: to admire a flower while there is a war on is not a politically insignificant act. Yet it would be equally extremist to insist that because art *can* be political, it must be. The more interesting question concerns the relation between a literary text and one or more of those 'sets of beliefs' which constitute an ideology.

1.9   Third, whose ideology are we interested in? The author's? The reader's? Or the text's (which may not be at all the same as the author's)? And what happens when, in the process of reading, these combine?

1.10   You will remember Stanley Fish's 'interpretive communities' from Block 3 Section 9. Does it now strike you that the members of such a community are likely to have some material interests in common, and hence a common ideological position which determines their interpretation? Do we (the students and teachers of the Open University) form such a community? We have in common a knowledge of the English language, an interest in literature and at least enough intelligence to cope with the system. But does that contribute more to our ideological point of view than our diversities? The story by Flannery O'Connor ('Revelation') may be a very different thing to the reader who shares her religious beliefs than to one who is indifferent or hostile. Indeed most of the authors discussed in this block are Roman Catholics or were raised in the Catholic tradition (even the Marxist Terry Eagleton). A religious ideology does not arise from a given set of *material interests*, of course, though religious practice frequently coincides with class divisions. So the spiritual, or 'non-material', interests of both author and reader are also parts of the ideological engagement.

1.11   Fourth, in what sense(s) is the production of literature an ideologically circumscribed act? We can see that both the writer and the reader are ideologically determined, but what about the apparently more mechanical aspects of literary production? Publication (the selection of what literature reaches the market-place) does not take place in an ideologically neutral context. This is the subject of TV7, which seeks to challenge the pleasantly romantic view that it is the idealized merit of a work of literature that determines its publication and survival. If you feel that it is incongruous to talk of literature in terms of production and consumption, this programme may change your mind. 'Literature', however, is only a small and relatively unprofitable proportion of the publishing trade's output. How does it survive in an age when – as the German novelist Günter Grass has put it – 'The book, formerly made to last forever, is beginning to resemble a non-returnable bottle' (1987)? Among such unrecyclable junk you might want to include the brick-sized bestsellers that even the snootiest of us sometimes read on holiday. These are certainly marketed like commodities. And what is their ideological significance? The thriller in which the good guys are invariably North American or British (and white and male) are not innocently apolitical, and the not-so-covert message of their feminine equivalents, politely known as Shopping and Fornicating novels, is that capitalism is the way to good sex.

1.12   Fifth, does literature perpetuate illusions? If, as Engels suggested, ideology is a false consciousness, does a text constitute the reflection of an ideology *and* its concomitant illusions? This more difficult question will be debated more extensively by Graham Martin in the second case-study, though it will also be raised in the second part of this introduction. Literary history is surely littered with illusions. Romantic love lyrics, for instance, conceal and perpetuate the material interests of men. But on the other hand, literature sometimes also seems able to 'tell the truth' about women's history even though readers have not always been able to see it. In literature, the sheer *absence* of women in so many of their roles has a lot to tell us about the values of the dominant ideology – and as you will see, it is in the scrutiny of gaps, absences and silences that much ideological significance has been located.

1.13   And sixth, is the very concept of 'literature' an ideological one? The notion of the 'canon' pervades this course. Why and how are certain works elected to that privileged status? What value-criteria are operating when we dub one work 'literature' and another merely 'fiction'? And what is the underlying political significance of *teaching* 'literature'? The humanist might claim that we are learning to appreciate the rare and beautiful; a more sceptical point of view might suggest that we are conspiring to preserve the status quo. This second idea achieved prominence among French Marxists in the late 1960s, when an alliance between students and the proletariat brought France close to revolution. As part of an attempt to analyse how oppression operates, Louis Althusser (see p.13) suggested that education, conventionally thought of as a liberating force, was actually an 'Ideological State Apparatus' (ISA) – one of the institutions through which the powerful interests in society perpetuate their hold. (This will be debated in Section 5, *'The Prime of Miss Jean Brodie'*.) In the hands of extremists this theory seems to me crass. I do not see literature as an agent of social control. But the idea is not to be dismissed because of its extreme forms – nor because of what *I* think. The Open University, for example, was founded and is funded by governments. How long would it survive if it *really* challenged the values of the state?

1.14   Everything you have so far read about the 'canon', the history of 'Eng. Lit.' and the notion of 'Englishness' will have revealed the political dimension in such issues. Traditionally, the study of literature was the study of the 'best' or the 'classics', and the 'canon' consisted of those texts that had secured a lasting respect. The overwhelming majority of these approved texts were written by white, middle-class men. In recent years, the loudest challenges to this complacent conspiracy have come from women, and from peoples and races outside the traditional centres of power: the challenges to what constitutes 'literature' are co-extensive with other challenges to European and North American orthodoxies. These are the themes of Blocks 6 and 7.

1.15   The primacy of English as an international language has survived the dissolution of a world-wide empire, thus perhaps giving the English an exaggerated sense of their importance in world affairs – and the superiority of their literature. If this had been a course on world literature the number of English authors would have been far smaller.

1.16   A translation from another language can be as powerful an influence on the literature of a particular country as any originating in that country's own language. Camus's *The Outsider* is an instance in this block. Literature can be international, though the distribution of the text, and hence the dissemination of its influence, is of course in the control of publishers and ultimately conditioned by trade. This is not, however, a course on world literature, but one on how the concept of English literature must shift in a changing world, and although that may seem an issue of little weight, it cannot be isolated from other questions of how we locate and define ourselves in the international community.

## Marxism and ideology

*1.17*   The set text for this section is a chapter from Terry Eagleton's short introductory work *Marxism and Literary Criticism* (1976). We have not included this text because we necessarily want you to endorse a Marxist perspective, but because Marxism is the only body of theory to attempt a consistent and systematic analysis of how literature and ideology are related. Nor could anyone properly claim to have a full view of how literature is studied today without knowing something of the basic tenets of Marxism and their application to literary studies. Terry Eagleton's chapter provides some basic, essential information, and you will be asked to read it section by section in conjunction with the notes, debating points and exercises set out below.

*1.18*   In a passage that is not included in the Reader extract, Eagleton postulates a Utopian socialist future: he speaks of 'the Communist society … where unlimited resources will serve an unlimitedly developing man', and of the 'measure between man and Nature which capitalist society necessarily destroys, and which socialist society can reproduce at an incomparably higher level'. It is specially important to pay attention to a writer's dates and historical circumstances when addressing the topics of this block. Eagleton's work was first published in 1976 when Britain had a Labour government. I am writing this in 1990, shortly after Poland, Hungary, East Germany, Czechoslovakia, Romania and Bulgaria have all rejected the single party state, and today's paper tells me that, far from having achieved any 'measure' between 'man and Nature', East Germany, for example, has the highest sulphur dioxide emission rate of any country in the world. What the political map will look like when *you* read this, I cannot guess.

*1.19*   My point is not to try and prove Eagleton wrong, and certainly not to crow about the present discomfiture of Communism. First of all, we have to distinguish Marxism from Communism, and while the latter may be in disarray, the theory with which it has always had a problematic relationship is not disproved. Perhaps Christianity in all its forms and churches bears a comparable relationship to the teachings of Christ. Just as institutionalized Christianity depends not so much on the gospels as on the continuing exegesis of them, so Marxism does not depend solely on what Marx and Engels said, but on how their words have been interpreted by their followers.

*1.20*   For many people the attractions of Marxism are not solely that it indicates how a more just society might be achieved, but also that it does so without any call on God. The influence of Christianity has declined throughout the twentieth century, but it has left behind an intellectually unsatisfactory residuum of half-beliefs and references to supernatural entities. Marxism on the other hand demands a radical atheism: we shall be looking at the opposition between materialism and essentialism in the next sub-section. At first sight, this may not seem to have much to do with the study of literature. But the production and status of 'high art' have frequently been described in terms that suggest a blurring between artistic and divine creation, and whenever a work of art is invoked in even the vaguest of mystic terms, a reference to the supernatural is implicitly involved. Marxists, on the other hand, would say that, as there is no God, and the material world and our labour is all we have, then in order to achieve a homogeneity of belief we must rid our thinking *entirely* of all God-substitutes. We cannot consistently allow the last traces of belief in a supernatural order to linger in our thinking about art and literature.

*ACTIVITY*

Please read the first paragraph of Eagleton's 'Marxist criticism' in the Reader
(p.207).

*1.21*  I doubt if it is true any longer that 'most students … are taught [that]
the greatest art is that which timelessly transcends its historical conditions'.
Open University students certainly aren't. In this 'transcendental' view of art
lurked the supernatural presences discussed above. The opposite position has
been expressed even more emphatically by Pierre Macherey, whose ideas you
will be debating when you study Camus's *The Outsider*:

> The literary work must be studied in a double perspective: in relation to
> history, and in relation to an ideological version of that history.
>
> (quoted in Wall, 1978)

*ACTIVITY*

Now read the second section, 'Base and superstructure' (Reader, pp.207–9).
Pay particular attention to the concluding sentences of both the long
quotations (pp.207–8):

(a)  'Consciousness does not determine life: life determines consciousness.'

(b)  'It is not the consciousness of men that determines their being, but on the
contrary, their social being that determines their consciousness.'

It is on these tenets that the 'materialist' position is based. 'Materialist' is
frequently used as a term of abuse by the high-minded, but I mean simply all
transactions involving resources, goods and labour *of any kind*. 'Essentialist' on
the other hand is a term that covers all theories that presuppose another, non-
material dimension to existence. The most common 'essence' is God in any of
his or her forms, but any notion of a value that transcends the material also
involves a notional 'essence'. It is part of an essentialist position that the non-
material is superior to the grossness of the material, and this has lead to the
right-wing slander that Marxism concerns itself only with the lowest common
denominator. (Eagleton refutes this in his third section.) In fact, Marx included
*all* kinds of human activity in his concept of labour and saw the impact on the
external world of all forms of labour (including thought) as fundamentally
creative.

The repetition of the word 'determines' in these key sentences is a useful
reminder that 'determinism' is another fundamental, but much
misunderstood, concept in Marxist philosophy. It does not refer to a totally
slavish and mechanical obedience to material laws. What Marx claimed was
that we are all born into a pre-existing social order, which inevitably shapes
our perceptions and sets limits to our freedoms, though we can never be fully
aware of how these restrictions act upon us.

In the full text, Eagleton concludes this section with the assertion that 'Marxist
criticism … sees that, in the absence of genuine revolutionary art, only a
radical conservatism, hostile like Marxism to the withered values of liberal
bourgeois society, could produce the most significant literature'.

*ACTIVITY*

How far can the principles implied here be applied to what you know of
Yeats, Eliot and Lawrence?

*DISCUSSION*

I expect you'd agree that all three are 'hostile ... to the withered values of
liberal bourgeois society' – but, put like this, who is not? Kipling, whose story
'A Sahibs' War' comes next in this block, is commonly thought of as a
mouthpiece for the dominant ideology of his period, and yet – well, you must
judge. In fact, it is really quite difficult to find examples of a durable literature
that is not 'hostile' to some degree. Perhaps the readiest examples of its
opposite – what we might call *complacent* literature – are to be found in
popular romances and thrillers, which have swallowed the dominant ideology
lock, stock and barrel. But probably the most 'popular' instance on this course
so far, the P. G. Wodehouse story, while not exactly 'hostile' is far from
complacent.

Did you find the phrase 'radical conservatism' equally appropriate to all three
authors? And if the term can be stretched to include Lawrence, with his
different class origins and his different political agenda, alongside Eliot and
Yeats, then is it too broad a classification to be useful? Who, by this standard,
could not lay claim to this ostensibly paradoxical title? In the scope of a
longer piece Eagleton would undoubtedly unpack these generalizations in
more detail.

*ACTIVITY*

Now read Eagleton's third section, 'Literature and superstructure' (Reader,
pp.209–13).

*1.22*   Neither Marx nor Engels ever made a simple equation between artistic
production and manufacture – look back to explanation (iii), quoted from
A102 in paragraph 1.2, and the fourth point on p.8. But Marxism certainly has
sought to relate artistic production to other forms of material and economic
endeavour, and challenges the essentialist view (here caricatured for brevity)
that art is created when inspiration breathes upon genius. This ignores the
artist's labour (we do after all speak of a *work* of art), the publishing process
and the vital role of the consumer or reader. Producing a novel may be as
much like setting up a small business as it is like receiving the divine afflatus,
and if we feel that the novel is denigrated by such a comparison, might not
that be because the value-system of our ideology has taught us to disparage
commerce while making us utterly dependent upon it? Think too of the
different kinds of work and the economics involved in the production of a
play.

*1.23*   I wonder if you were satisfied by Eagleton's answer to the question
about why Greek art (or indeed any art not of our time) should still give us
pleasure? Brecht's response is surely hardly an 'answer' even if we agree that
it is indeed a 'sensual delight' – or at least a pleasure – to recognize the
familiar combined with the distant and alien in the artefacts of the past.
Common sense alone would suggest that a literary text cannot be entirely
autonomous ('self-governing'). It must have some relationship to the historical
conditions in which it was produced. Experience on the other hand suggests
that there is no simple quasi-algebraic formula that would enable us to

calculate what historical input produces what literary results. And, as Brecht maintains, the pleasure (you could also say the *interest*, even the *meaningfulness*) of an artefact can (though not always) outlast its own time by thousands of years. To account for this, Marxists have evolved theories of 'relative autonomy'. There is no need to go into this in detail, though the term is worth remembering and we shall return to it in Section 9. It suggests that not only is the relationship between the arts and the economic/material base variable, but that works of art can influence their successors directly without the unmediated influence of the base.

*1.24*  Eagleton takes *The Waste Land* as an example of how much a sophisticated Marxist analysis can reveal when an artefact is scrutinized not merely for its relation to the prevailing economic base, but for its precise location within the complexities of the superstructure. The point to grasp is that there is no Marxist rule of thumb, and certainly no formulaic Marxist mincer through which the processed artefact is extruded, neat and predictable as a sausage. It is another common slander that Marxism is the enemy of difference, uniqueness and individuality. Though they are by no means all written by Marxists, the case-studies which follow in this block will try to exemplify some of this complexity.

## ACTIVITY

Look back to work you have already done and, using as a guide the questions implied in Eagleton's approach to *The Waste Land*, ask similar questions of either *England Made Me* or *Officers and Gentlemen*.

## DISCUSSION

You do not have much information about the authors of course, but the Catholicism of both surely alienated them from a largely lapsed Protestant society? Then the time of writing is significant. In the early 30s Greene sees the Nazis coming to power and the English national character as morally bankrupt. I wonder if you felt that the theme of incest suggested a nation too dangerously self-absorbed to be effective? Waugh on the other hand is looking backwards, though not to glory. One of the crucial absences that I mentioned in paragraph 1.12 is surely *the enemy*.

## ACTIVITY

Now read the fourth section of Eagleton's 'Marxist criticism', subtitled 'Literature and ideology' (Reader, pp.213–15).

*1.25*  Perhaps you would not agree with the word 'precise' in the second sentence: 'it is important here to grasp the precise meaning for Marxism of "ideology".' We saw in the previous subsection that 'ideology' was used in two senses by Marx himself. Now a further development is suggested: 'ideology … signifies the way men *live out their roles*.'

*1.26*  This is very important. It derives from Althusser's very influential definition:

> Ideology represents the imaginary relationship of individuals to their real conditions of existence.
>
> (Althusser, 1983, p.36)

*1.27*   We started off thinking of ideology as 'a set of beliefs' – which suggests *thought*. Now it's being put to you that it is how we *live* – though in some 'imaginary' way, which Eagleton suggests is analogous to our experience of art: we 'read' our lives as we might read a novel. Obviously there's a lot that needs unpacking here, but Eagleton himself admits to finding Althusser (who was a philosopher, not a literary critic) difficult, so take heart. A familiar example may help. If a professed socialist sends his or her children to a private school, then their *lived* ideology belies what they proclaim, and in the material world the lived has a real impact on the state provision whereas the theory is only so much hot air. The lived is what matters, conscious or not. Althusser states that 'ideology has a material existence' (ibid., p.36). But in what relationship can the 'imaginary' and the 'material' be aligned? Althusser suggests, in his rather unpolished jottings, that we can easily recognize the imaginary in 'world outlooks' or ideologies we do *not* share:

> We commonly call religious ideology, ethical ideology, legal ideology, political ideology, etc., so many 'world outlooks'. Of course, assuming that we do not live one of these ideologies as the truth (e.g. 'believe' in God, Duty, Justice, etc. …). We admit that the ideology we are discussing from a critical point of view, examining it as the ethnologist examines the myths of a 'primitive society', that these 'world outlooks' are largely imaginary, i.e. do not 'correspond to reality'.

> However, while admitting that they do not correspond to reality, i.e. that they constitute an illusion, we admit that they do make allusion to reality, and that they need only be 'interpreted' to discover the reality of the world behind their imaginary representation of that world…

> (Ibid., p.36)

And he goes on to suggest that there is always an imaginary dimension in whatever outlooks or ideologies we may subscribe to, whether consciously or not. I mentioned earlier that the thinking (and the living) even of professed atheists may still be affected by residual religious beliefs or practices, which they do not recognize as such. And there are other ideologies, sometimes hard to name, which permeate our lives and make our actions contradict our thoughts. That we may be quite unaware of any contradiction takes us back to the idea of false consciousness, to which Eagleton refers later in this section. We are often aware of a sexism in earlier literature that its authors cannot have been aware of, because it was part of the general ideological air they breathed: we can refer to such beliefs as *lived or naturalized ideologies*. Similarly there is a degree of casual anti-semitism in much of the very 'best' literature up to the Second World War, which is now horrifying. More recently, white writers have become a little more sensitive to their own unconscious racism – though many of us are aware that beyond the prejudices which, with vigilance, we might identify, there are layers more, as yet beyond our reach.

*1.28*   Is it claiming too much to suggest that the study of literature can make our false consciousness slightly less 'false'? This is what I think Eagleton means when he says that:

> [Art] is held within ideology, but also manages to distance itself from it, to the point where it permits us to 'feel' and 'perceive' the ideology from which it springs.

> (Reader, p.214)

Speaking for myself, I don't think so. And if we gloss 'false' with Althusser's 'imaginary' or even think more simply of a 'partial' consciousness, then the assertion becomes less problematic. But *how* literature can show us things that we have not been able to deduce from life is another matter. Althusser said that realists 'make us *see, perceive* (but not know) something which *alludes* to reality' ('A Letter to André Daspre', 1966). But I would not want to restrict this power to literary realism: non-realist writers can make us see at least as clearly.

1.29   In the first case-study, by disinterring some of the layers of lived ideology in 'A Sahibs' War', I hope to show not that Kipling was a racist, but that the story reveals some of the half-hidden ways in which racism operates. This may thus prove a good example of how a literary text can 'make us see'.

1.30   And this is surely a more positive programme than may have been suggested to you by the rather negative tone of the sentence about *The Waste Land* in this section of Eagleton's essay. It is not the intention of any of the case-studies to clobber a text with its own ideological import.

## ACTIVITY

To conclude this section, and to link what follows with the set texts, test two or three of those texts you have already studied against the 'two extreme, opposite positions' that Eagleton outlines:

(a)   '…works of literature are just expressions of the ideologies of their time';

(b)   'Authentic art … always transcends the ideological limits of its time'.

## DISCUSSION

I raised similar questions at the opening of this section, and you will have guessed which way I incline. What I hope you will have concluded is that both positions are too extreme to be useful, and we need to proceed in a more subtle manner. In *Officers and Gentlemen*, for example, I find precious little transcendence of the prevailing ideology concerning women; but on the other hand that absence of 'the enemy' that I referred to above, suggests that the need to defeat Fascism was not quite the driving force that propagandists would have us believe and that Waugh (perhaps with the advantages of hindsight) 'transcended the ideological limits' by seeing that something was crumbling in the State of England. Indeed, would you not agree that although all the examples in Block 3 posit an idealized dream of England, they all equally include quite savage criticism of that ideal?

But it is now time to turn to this block's own case-studies and to leave England behind.

# 2   Kipling: 'A Sahibs' War'

2.1   Kipling's story of the Boer War takes us back to the heyday of British imperialism. Camus's *The Outsider* concerns Algeria under French rule. And Fugard, Kani and Ntshona's play *The Island* returns us to South Africa, once a 'British possession' and where the black and 'coloured' populations continue to live under a quasi-imperial domination. So we must briefly consider some of the ideologies of imperialism – especially as the *end* of Empire is the theme of Block 5. This block takes us away from England. Kipling is the only English author, though he pretends that the author of his story is Indian. In fact, you will notice that the block is arranged to begin with an Englishman imitating an Indian and ends with the authentic voices of black South Africa, partially mediated through the necessary agency of their co-author. And since this block contains two texts relating to South Africa, some historical contextualization is specially important.

*Dutch descended south african*

## South Africa and the Boer War, 1899–1902

*2.2*   What follows attempts to provide a narrative and to stress points of particular relevance to the text we shall be studying without, at this stage, being too tendentious, or trying to prejudice you. So read it carefully. When we are considering questions of ideology, the historical and political context is specially important.

*2.3*   The area around what is now Cape Town was first settled by the Dutch in the mid-seventeenth century. It is sometimes claimed that there was then no indigenous population to be displaced. In fact, rather as in Australia in the nineteenth century, the inhabitants were sparse and nomadic, and their culture was invisible to the newcomers. When the expanding Dutch populations began to move north in the eighteenth century they met and clashed with Bantu tribes migrating south from their original territories in central and eastern Africa. Between these black and white expansionist movements the aboriginal peoples were forced towards the Kalahari. Apologists for apartheid (which was not formulated as a policy until after the Second World War) frequently insisted that South Africa's present black population has no more entitlement to the land than they do, since both populations are descended from colonists.

*2.4*   The Dutch were well established before the British arrived in the early nineteenth century, and they were enraged when, without their consent, the Cape was formally ceded to Britain by the Dutch in 1814, after being captured in the Napoleonic wars. Although in 1820 some 5,000 British settlers arrived, they were a minority and naturally they were resented. In 1837 over 10,000 Boers embarked on the Great Trek northwards, to escape and found their own republics of the Orange Free State, Transvaal and Natal. It was an episode that combined in one event the revolutionary fervour of a war of independence with the pioneering grit of the wagon-trains; and the Bantu and the Zulu played the part the 'Red Indians' were to play in the American West. The heroic mythology of the Boers is a significant factor in subsequent Afrikaner history.

*2.5*   Perhaps the war that eventually broke out in 1899 was inevitable, as the two white populations exploited every chance of besting the other. From the British point of view a crucial issue was that of the 'Uitlanders', another generation of (mostly) British opportunists migrating to Boer-controlled territories, this time for the gold-rush to Witwatersrand in 1886. Kruger's Transvaal government allowed the outlanders no rights and no votes, but taxed them heavily, both on what they mined and the equipment they imported to get it. The Transvaal became rich, and Kruger began to arm. He flirted with Germany, even though his government was party to an agreement that prohibited any negotiation with a foreign power save through Britain.

*2.6*   Ranged against Kruger was Cecil Rhodes, the premier of Cape Province, who was, at first, supported by the Cape Dutch as well as the British. Rhodes was managing director of the Great Chartered Company, a trader and an adventurer, and his many friends in Britain included Kipling as well as politicians of most persuasions. He wanted – and it was very much a matter of personal ambition – to connect Cape Town to Rhodesia by rail. But to do so he needed a strip of land through Bechuanaland and Kruger's Transvaal. How he acquired it matters little here: he did – and with it the right to police the territory.

*S.A*
*1st Dutch*
*2nd English*

*2.7*   Rhodes then decided that he was going to use this police force as the basis of what was virtually a small private army to relieve the taxed but unrepresented Uitlanders of Johannesburg in what came to be known as the Jameson Raid. This was not only a grandiose and arrogant folly; it was also a breach of international law, since no formal state of war existed. Really, it was no better than an attempted hijack, but 'at home' in Britain it was reinterpreted as an heroic enterprise. When the Kaiser sent a telegram to the Transvaal government congratulating them on their defeat of the raiders, patriotic sentiments in Britain were roused. It was the first sign that Victoria's German grandson might not always be Britain's friend. Kipling's 'Hymn before Action' contributed to the mood:

> The earth is full of anger,
>    The seas are dark with wrath,
> The nations in their harness
>    Go up against our path:
> Ere yet we loose the legions
>    Ere yet we draw the blade,
> Jehovah of the Thunders,
>    Lord God of Battles, aid!

The Kaiser's intervention made the British government less inclined to chastise Rhodes. During the enquiry in London, Rhodes managed to prevent the committee seeing certain telegrams sent to the Cape before the raid and this roused suspicions in London – and convictions in Dutch South Africa – that Chamberlain, who was Colonial Secretary, must have known of, or encouraged, this preposterous *Boys' Own* adventure. Chamberlain certainly made the situation worse by declaring in Parliament that nothing Rhodes had done affected his 'personal position as a man of honour'. If heroic myths were a crucial ingredient in the Boer version of South African history, they were no less important to the British. Rhodes had enjoyed the support of the Dutch as well as the British at the Cape. In squandering his Dutch allies he fatally jeopardized any hope of unity between the two white races.

*2.8*   It is all too likely that any history of South Africa you come across will be written – just as this digest is – from a white point of view. It's easy to believe that, at this time, the tides of white history simply flowed around the blacks, though, as I'm sure you will realize, an account of this period written from a black point of view would be very different. A glimpse of this different history is afforded by the 1896 rebellion in Matabeleland which was made possible by the absence of the mounted police who had been seconded to the raiders. From the British standpoint the episode is remarkable for Colonel Baden-Powell's scoutcraft against the guerrillas and for the manner in which Rhodes almost single-handedly managed to penetrate the Matabele stronghold and parley their chiefs to a surrender. It was the same Baden-Powell of course who went on to found the Boy Scouts, and Rhodes's heroism was reconfirmed. For the British public these were ripping yarns. The Matabele must have felt differently.

*2.9*   Public opinion played a considerable part in driving the British government to war. Late in 1898 a British workman (an Uitlander) called Tom Edgar was shot dead by a Johannesburg policeman – who was acquitted by a Boer jury. Uitlander protests were harshly repressed, and a petition with the signatures of over 20,000 British citizens of the Rand was sent to the Queen. To have ignored it would have signalled that Britain was indifferent to the fate of its citizens overseas and the sentiments of patriots at home. 'Though the cabinet of Great Britain was not bellicose', comments R.C.K. Ensor (1936, p.250), 'a large and noisy section of her people were … If the Boers became united by the mistaken conviction that a British government wanted their blood, it was largely because they heard a British public calling for it.' But the Boers were not only arming for a defensive war. They believed the whole country should be theirs by right of majority and longer settlement. The British, on the other hand, were intent on unifying the South African states under British rule, even though they had hoped to achieve this by settlement rather than war.

*2.10* They 'won' of course, and this fact has had a distorting influence on British views of South Africa ever since. The white populations have never united and certainly never been whole-heartedly pro-British. But really, considering the disasters of the first part of the campaign, it is surprising that they won at all. It was a chronicle of mismanagement.

*2.11* The self-governing white colonies all sent large voluntary detachments – a significant precedent for both world wars. As they saw it, the crux of the war was Britain's defence of its overseas nationals. But 'native' Indian troops were deliberately excluded. In the words of a young Boer guerrilla, there was 'an unwritten law that this was a white man's quarrel, and that the native tribes were to be left alone' (Reitz, 1929). The ethics of the day made it unthinkable that black men should be called upon to fire on whites, so the British voluntarily tied one arm behind their backs by not deploying their most experienced troops. Ensor, moreover, suggests that even the lessons learned in India were misapplied:

> ... the generals went ahead with the tactics usual on the Indian frontier: uphill frontal infantry attacks, which had done well enough against Afridis or Afghans, but were useless against armies of white marksmen armed with Mauser rifles.
>
> (Ensor, op. cit., p.293)

The British tried to fight an old-fashioned war, not fully realizing that the Boers were struggling for what they saw as their homeland. Though the British had vastly superior numbers and equipment, they were constantly harassed by guerrilla tactics and what they saw as the treachery of the civilian population. A war, they piously believed, was the business only of uniformed troops. In fact, the greatest casualties of the war were civilians: the women and children who died of fever in the concentration camps (the first use of this sinister term) where they had been mustered by the British 'for their own good'. The peace, when it came, was by negotiation.

## Rudyard Kipling (1865–1936)

*2.12* Rudyard Kipling was born in Bombay to a middle-class English family which had 'connections' with both artistic and political circles in Britain. His mother was related to Sir Edward Burne-Jones and other pre-Raphaelite painters and writers, and the politician Stanley Baldwin (1867–1947) was a cousin. Kipling's father Lockwood was a professor at the school of art, a man devoted to the cause of Indian arts and crafts.

*2.13* Like most Anglo-Indian children, Rudyard was sent 'home' at the age of six, first for five miserable years with relatives, then to public school – in Kipling's case a rather rough and ready establishment called Westward Ho! (the exclamation mark is part of the name). He returned to India without going to university, became a journalist, started to write short stories – at first mainly about India – and became very famous before he was twenty-five. He left India in 1889, and after a visit in 1891 never returned. He married a North American (a long but not easy marriage), and spent much of the next decade living in Vermont. He travelled extensively, and from 1900 to 1908 spent every winter near Cape Town – that is, the pro-British part of South Africa. Fame, a useful family, and an enthusiastic personality had gained him a large circle of friends in all kinds of high places – including Cecil Rhodes, who gave the Kiplings a house on his own estate. It was there that he wrote much of the *Just So Stories* and *Puck of Pook's Hill*.

2.14   Kipling is one of those figures whose name has a meaning to far more people than know his work. Above all, he is associated with British imperialism. In her book *The Origins of Totalitarianism* Hannah Arendt wrote:

> The author of the imperial legend is Rudyard Kipling, its topic the British Empire, its result the imperialist character ... and chivalry, nobility, bravery answered the legend's call ... Imperialism was a chance to escape a society in which a man had to forget his youth if he wanted to grow up.
>
> (Arendt, 1958, pp.208–10)

Notice the references to legendary virtues which even a critic of imperialism cannot avoid citing, however ironically. Where we see exploitation in the situation, contemporaries saw a fairer exchange: preferential trading terms for good government. That white races were superior was part of the naturalized ideology: hardly any European had ever thought any differently and the fact that the Chinese (for example) believed that *they* were naturally superior was rather a joke.

2.15   Although of course the basis of the empire was commercial, this fact was largely ignored by the imperialists with their typically British disdain for trade. (Perhaps the same phenomenon is what makes so many middle-class British reluctant to take Marxism seriously: they cannot quite bring themselves to believe that everything – but everything – has a *material* basis.)

2.16   For the middle classes, as the quotation from Arendt suggests, imperialism was fun. The young white male in the Indian Civil Service, for example, was rewarded for his hard work with good sport, a high standard of living, and – even some of Kipling's stories acknowledge this – exotic women. (The female imperialist will come under consideration in the next block.) The literature suggests that the risk of sudden death was the price to be paid, but sudden death was in any case a familiar phenomenon. Perhaps it was the sudden *funeral* necessitated by tropical or equatorial climes that was more disturbing to the Victorian imagination. Or maybe – I suspect this of Kipling – the emphasis on ever-imminent fever and death helps to enhance the *machismo.* Few imperialists were conscious sadists, going out to tread down the natives. If they felt guilt (and there is a distinct shiftiness in 'A Sahibs' War', which we shall discuss later), it may have less to do with any inherent immorality in the endeavour than with a puritan mistrust of pleasure.

2.17   Kipling's brand of imperialism has been summed up by his biographer Charles Carrington thus:

> No man had done more than Kipling to stimulate interest in the opening-up of new worlds in the east and south. He never doubted the validity of western civilization, never lapsed into sentiment over the supposed virtues of savages; but it was the spread of law, literacy, communications, useful arts that he applauded, not the enlargement of frontiers ... Civilizing the world was a worthwhile task, and though likely to be thankless, a task in which all might join if they would accept the law. Rhodes, in his chastened mood after the failure of the Jameson raid, was fully occupied with agricultural reform at the Cape, with railway construction in Rhodesia, with land settlement, with the Cape-to-Cairo telegraph ... Rhodes, immersed in plans for material progress rather than in politics, was the leader Kipling adhered to.
>
> (Carrington, 1955, p.332)

Carrington's own ideological colours are showing here of course. He was a soldier as well as an historian, and a professor of commonwealth relations; and his book was published on the eve of Suez. But he was right to point out that imperialism and an aggressive expansionism were not inseparable. Kipling was far from enchanted by military glamour. Indeed, in well known poems such as *The Widow of Windsor* and some of his greatest stories, he showed how the whole enterprise was carried on the long-suffering backs of the enlisted men and their women. Few of his generation had seen active service, of course, so perhaps many were particularly susceptible to heroism. Kipling's attitude to war is exemplified by a couplet from *The Second Jungle Book*:

> When Pack meet Pack in the Jungle, and neither will go from the
>     trail,
> Lie down till the leaders have spoken – it may be fair words will
>     prevail.

*2.18*  In 1900, the second year of the war, Kipling was invited to work for the troops' newspaper in Cape Town, and this gave him one opportunity to see action at first hand. Presumably the skirmish he was taken to see was not particularly perilous: it would have been embarrassing to have lost such a celebrity. But the account he wrote of it in his autobiography thirty years later (*Something of Myself* was published in 1937) is wonderfully vivid:

> The enormous pale landscape swallowed up seven thousand troops without a sign … There was a decent lull for meals on both sides, interrupted now and again by sputters. Then one indubitable shell – ridiculously like a pip-squeak in the vastness but throwing up much dirt … Every twenty minutes or so, one judgmatic shell pitched on our slope. We waited, seeing nothing in the emptiness, and hearing only a faint murmur as of wind along gas-jets, running in and out of the unconcerned hills …

The following year a bizarre story appeared in a Geneva newspaper. It alleged that Kipling had taken part in the murder of a civilian on this excursion, and that he had written it up with unseemly relish. According to Carrington, the continental newspapers were full of anti-British propaganda at the time. Kipling retorted that the propagandist was seeing the 'reflection of his own face as he spied at our back window'. But you may think that when he wrote 'A Sahibs' War' in December 1901, he came close to fulfilling the accusation. Kipling enjoyed a film-star celebrity in his time: not only did everything he wrote achieve instant and wide circulation; but everything he did or said, and every jot of gossip about him, was news.

## ACTIVITY

'A Sahibs' War' (Prose Anthology, pp.6–24) is a complicated story and you will need to read it at least twice, and certainly once now before going on.

Now look back to paragraphs 1.6–1.13, where I have suggested six ways of considering the relationship between a literary text and ideology. Using this list, try to formulate some brief preliminary thoughts on the ideological questions pertinent to this text.

## DISCUSSION

(i)   As Kipling was a well-known patriot, a story of his about the Boer War would seem likely to be written 'for the cause'. But is it? I expect we can agree that this is not an anti-war tale, but it is savagely contemptuous of official policies and management, in particular the decision not to use Indian troops.

(ii)   Some of Kipling's best known works are his fantasies for children, but otherwise it might be said that he used his writing to participate in political life. This would seem to make him an anti-Modernist (and indeed there was no love lost between him and Bloomsbury) but the story is distinctly Modernist in its techniques.

(iii) Kipling was a popular author, writing about a popular war, which had indeed partly been brought about by popular feeling. You might therefore expect a comfortable, complacent story that would exactly match the mood of the times. But you can hardly have missed its tone of contempt, and giving the story a Sikh narrator deliberately prevents his white British readers identifying with the teller, while at the same time proclaiming *'this is not Kipling speaking'*.

(iv) Kipling was in the privileged position of being able to publish very easily anything he wrote. Because of his reputation it was assumed that everything he wrote was patriotic. You may well wonder (especially if you come to this course via A102) whether his was the voice of the 'dominant ideology'.

(v) The story debunks some illusions but sustains others: we'll go into this in more detail later.

(vi) Kipling is certainly canonical now. But his status has an interesting history. His popularity was enough to damn him among his more refined contemporaries. Bloomsbury considered him a vulgar fascist, and when T.S. Eliot (by no means a left-winger) introduced an anthology of his poetry (called *A Choice of Kipling's 'Verse'*), this was the charge he felt bound to defend his subject against. George Orwell, writing in an essay published in 1942, felt he was in many respects indefensible:

> It is no use pretending that Kipling's view of life as a whole, can be accepted or even forgiven by any civilized person … He does not see the map is painted red chiefly in order that the coolie may be exploited. Instead of the coolie he sees the Indian Civil Servant; but even on that plan his grasp of function, of who protects who, is very sound. He sees clearly that men can only be highly civilized while other men, inevitably less civilized, are there to guard and feed them.
>
> (Orwell, 1942)

In the same essay Orwell betrayed some of his own ideological blind spots by 'restoring the aitches' in Kipling's careful dialect spellings. But though he despised him, he was obliged to acknowledge Kipling's power. Eliot's anthology, he suggested, was a confession 'to a taste which others share but are not always honest enough to mention'. Enjoying him, he felt was 'almost a shameful pleasure, like a taste for cheap sweets that some people secretly carry into middle life'. In the years after his death, Kipling's work was considered by the intelligentsia to be no better than a kind of political pornography, alluring but reprehensible. He was refused the status of an artist, and his popularity was seen as the mark of the beast.

## ACTIVITY

You should now have read the story once, and the background information I have provided. I should like you to read it again more carefully, using the following notes for explication and to build up a more complex appreciation of the story, which will be debated in general in the rest of this section. You will remember that in Section 1, I referred to the ideology of the *reader*. It is important to remember that you have yours and I have mine. I have tried to postpone persuading you to my view of this story until you are in a position of some strength, but of course it is an intrinsic feature of unconscious, lived ideologies that a value-free neutrality is impossible, so you may well feel that you have already been preconditioned to some extent. We shall be looking at the explicit ideology of the story (that is to say, the political points Kipling is deliberately making) and the implicit 'lived' ideologies, which may in some instances contradict or subvert the surface. *This contrast, between the explicit and the implicit, the overt and the hidden, the proclaimed and the lived, the 'witting' and the 'unwitting' will be a feature of all the cases studies in this block.*

## A study guide to 'A Sahibs' War'

### The title

*2.19*   This tells the whole story in brief, and becomes an ironic and bitter refrain. The word 'sahib' seems to be derived from the Arabic word for 'friend'. If so, it now contains a colossal historical irony, since to us it epitomizes an authoritarian relationship between the white rulers and the black indigenous people they governed. It means the boss class and, as we have seen, there was a gentlemen's agreement that the war should be limited to the sahibs. *But, the story goes on to suggest, the sahib ethos will never win it.*

### Language

*2.20*   The story purports to be told by a Sikh member of an Indian cavalry regiment – in which only the officers were British. The Hindu words and phrases and the transliterations such as *rêl*, *terain* and *Ustrelyahs* (Australians) keep reminding us that we are to imagine him telling the story in his own language to one 'sahib' who can translate it for another. Despite the closeness of his relationship with his particular sahib – whose very name is quite different on Umr Singh's tongue – he speaks no English. *This suggests an intimacy that went only one way.*

*2.21*   The story is so packed with exotic place names that we feel we are reading a half-understood code. The word *Hind* means literally the area where Hindu is spoken. But in the phrase 'It is for Hind' it stands for the imperialist idea that prevails there, or the Raj.

*2.22*   'The long war in the Tirah' is a reference to the North West Frontier campaign, where the officially excluded Indian regiments learnt their anti-guerrilla skills. Umr Singh says '*We* could have done it all so gently' (ponder that last word as well as the 'we', which draws in the reader) but, as Ensor suggested, it may be that, in fact, the lessons of the Tirah, when applied to the South African campaign, proved disastrous. Kipling thought the campaign was mismanaged but his own inexpert advice, proffered through this story, was not necessarily right.

*2.23*   And yet what he writes *sounds* so expert. The foreign words are part of the very jargon of empire. Using an in-group's slang is a way of assuming their values, and it can draw the reader into the conspiracy, though perhaps we are too far distant for that particular trick to work. The story is quite candid about what it is trying to do: we are supposed to imagine that the narrator is addressing a sahib 'born and bred in Hind'.

### Race and caste

*2.24*   As we have seen, the war pretended to be 'a white man's quarrel', but a glimpse of blatant racism in the first paragraph suggests that at some level Kipling knew that race was an inescapable part of the issue. The narrator, Umr Singh, thinks he is a cut above 'these black Kaffirs' whom he later refers to in even more unpleasant terms. He thrashes the 'Mussulman pig' and takes his place as Kurban Sahib's servant. He will sacrifice military rank, caste and even religious principles in the white man's service, but not his innate sense of superiority, which is at least partially derived from his privileged proximity to the British army:

> ... I, a Sikh of the Khalsa, an unshorn man, prepared the razors. But I did not put on my uniform while I did it. On the other hand, Kurban Sahib took for me, upon the steamer, a room in all respects like to his own, and would have given me a servant.
>
> (Prose Anthology, p.10)

Later, notice his attitude to Sikandar Khan. Racial distinctions indicate power relationships. Does Kipling approve? His personal views are hidden behind a narrative device which allows him to express racism without owning to it. Indeed, the story seems to be claiming that it is not the whites who are racist (Kurban Sahib treats his bearer like a buddy) but the *blacks*. Again, this is the parade of insider expertise: racism was, and is, a political factor in the subcontinent. Hannah Arendt emphasizes the pervasiveness of racism among the imperialists, but really it seems to be a phenomenon as regrettably universal as sexism.

2.25  Of course the language has done its best to persuade the reader that this is how a Sikh *really* feels, and thus to accept his surely nauseating deference as natural and idiomatic. There is nothing *imposed* about this Heaven-born palaver, the narrative seems to say, the chap's boss couldn't be fairer. And Kipling is alert to some of the paradoxes in the situation: 'when we were alone he called me Father, and I called him Son.' This actually inverts the more public formulation of the myth: the Great White Father and his native children. (Victoria was often referred to as the *Mother*-empress.) That the colonial relationship is a dependency is obvious; but what Kipling is trying to suggest is that each side was equally dependent on the other: this was the dominant ideology's agreeable fiction, and here, it seems, is an Indian backing it up.

**The war**

2.26  The subject of the paragraph beginning 'We spoke about this war' should be clear to you from the discussion on page 17: the plight of the Uitlanders and the death of Tom Edgar. But look carefully at the passage beginning: 'He said, "They have taken men afoot..."' (p.10). Really, if we understand it, it is because we are still party to the imperialist complicity. It takes some unpicking. The 'Boer-log' are white, of course, but it is implied that in a metaphorical sense they are not, i.e. not upright, decent, trustworthy fellows. If they were literally black, the passage quite frankly suggests, no holds would be barred, and vengeance *would* be taken. And that, the story suggests, is how the war should have been fought: civilian informers ought to have been executed as they were in Burma or Kabul – 'schooled', or even more euphemistically 'pushed off the verandah' (hanged). Indeed, Kipling had a point. The war was certainly prolonged because of the ill-fated but well-intentioned policy of civilian internment, which meant that the British army was provisioning enemy dependants as well as its own troops. He has identified a double standard and it is both shrewd and duplicitous of him to express it through an Indian. In effect, telling an unpalatable truth is just one more of the dirty jobs the sahibs need their colonial servants to perform for them.

2.27  Kipling admired expertise, and was contemptuous of amateurishness, bungling and ineptitude: '...new Sahibs from God knows where ... full of zeal, but empty of all knowledge' (p.11). Scorn brings out some of his most fiery writing. This was the last cavalry war, fought over immense fronts, and the British poured in prodigious numbers of horses: 'God knows what the army did with them, unless they ate them raw. They used horses as a courtesan uses oil: with both hands...' (p.11) – a wonderfully inexplicit simile that suggests an untold depravity of extravagance.

2.28   Another 'new brand of sahib' are the white colonials, the Canadian and the Australian volunteers, the *Durro Muts*: 'Dark, tall men, most excellent horsemen, hot and angry, waging war *as* war, and drinking tea as a sandhill drinks water' (p.13).

2.29   His admiration here is as plain as his contempt elsewhere, and since the war was fought largely for the sake of the new white colonials, as we have seen, Kipling's praise declares that they were worth fighting for. The one quality they lack is subtlety: it is 'some fool of the *Durro Muts*' who fails to understand that the exchange between Kurban Sahib and Umr Singh about 'over-many cooks in the cook house' is a warning about the hidden gunners, and so brings down the ambush. The old world traditionally claims that it is more expert in craft, cunning and sophistry than the new.

2.30   The ugly, powerful cliché that pervades the ambush and the Indians' planned revenge is the idea that, because the Boers didn't behave like 'white men' (i.e. didn't restrict the fighting to their uniformed battalions), they did not deserve to be treated like white men.

**The ambush and its aftermath**

2.31   This is an episode that demands detailed attention. First, why do you think Kipling made the Boer family so repulsive?

2.32   Do you remember the Great Trek, referred to in paragraph 2.4 of this block? Kipling has stripped these Boers of all their pioneering heroism. The effect is a bit like those debunking Westerns where the cowboy is revealed in his dingy, drooping combinations. He makes them collectively brutal ('The swine's eyes and the jowl of a swine', p.20), idiotic and diseased – even syphilitic. Dehumanizing the enemy is of course a classic strategy for propagandists. Had they been merely ordinary, we might have remembered more quickly that whether their actions were treacherous or not depends on your point of view.

2.33   The episode is frankly sadistic. The woman 'pawing' at Umr Singh's boots is a figure out of jack-boot pornography. But it is just as susceptible to literary analysis as any less ambiguously pleasurable effect of language.

*ACTIVITY*

Look at the passage describing Kurban Sahib's death ('Be still. It is a Sahibs' war', p.18) and try to distinguish the variety of tones.

*DISCUSSION*

Among them is the silence indicated by the row of stops – a very manly, tearless silence, though hardly an 'English' silence. It is stately ('and at the drinking his spirit received permission'), ritualistic and with a touch of Eastern mystique. At the same time there is a soldierly ethic, which purports to be unsentimental but wrings the withers just the same: 'I gave him water that he might pass the more quickly.'

Kipling's prose lopes effortlessly over a huge variety of tones. The floridly rhetorical ('...he was a butler and would light the table, and I looked for a branch that would bear fruit') contrasts with *machismo* understatement: 'It was a very pretty stroke – for a Pathan.' His thumb is most obviously in the scale

– he is at his most manipulative – when he brings in shades of the Bible, not just *thou* and *thee* and *thy*, but phrases such as 'praised among men and loved among women' and the 'third cockcrow' (p.21), which dares to link the order of betrayal here with Peter denying Christ. But Umr Singh's ethic is closer to the Old Testament – 'eye for an eye' – than the New. Biblical, too, is the repeated connection of phrase to phrase with 'and', and the use of 'and' to open a succession of sentences, as it does when the ghost exhorts them with quasi-liturgical repetition to remember that 'It is a Sahibs' war'. The effect of these overtones is to suggest that the government of empire is a religious duty.

2.34   We have seen that contrary to what we might have expected from a famous patriot, 'A Sahibs' War' is fiercely critical, yet obliquely expressed. Kipling belongs in that very English tradition of angry conservatives who see around them a failure to live up to a Utopian ideal, which they believe could be quite easily achieved if only everyone would put their shoulders to the same wheel. And he is scathingly contemptuous of liberal compromise. Some famous lines from *The Islanders* (1902) make his feelings plain:

> And ye vaunted your fathomless power, and ye flaunted your iron
>    pride,
> Ere ye fawned on the Younger Nations for men who could shoot and
>    ride!
> Then ye returned to your trinkets; then ye contented your souls
> With the flannelled fools at the wicket or the muddied oafs at the
>    goals.

But the complexities of his narrative technique obscure some of the flaws in his argument as we can see if we probe deeper, to where the unconscious ideologies are at work. I want to consider two topics: the construction of the sahib and the issue of race.

**The 'sahib'**

*ACTIVITY*

'One effect of Kipling's narrative technique is that it prevents us from seeing Kurban Sahib too clearly; and that is an advantage, for if we did see what the story reveals, we should realize that the empire's idol is a sham.'

Consider this, then skim the story again looking for evidence to confirm or refute it; and do not forget the significant omissions.

*DISCUSSION*

I wonder if you included silence among his characteristics? His speech is seldom reported and his presence in the narrative is swamped by Umr Singh's volubility. This is surely racial stereotyping: the natives do run on so, but the Englishman is silent. He cannot talk – in his own English – about honour, patriotism, his women-folk or God, all of which he would die defending. This silence is perhaps particularly apparent in the understated way in which he is – belatedly – endowed with a sexual identity: he was 'loved among women' (p.21) and his silk handkerchiefs were 'given him by a certain woman' (p.23). The two phrases between them attribute to him both a legendary virility ('among women') and a proper gentlemanly devotion to one woman in particular. Only a very dimly realized character can contain such opposites easily.

He is a very conventional young man whose only claim to Umr Singh's servile devotion (other than his race, of course) is the apparent equality he offers: 'We spoke freely together on everything – about war, and women, and money…' (p.8). Notice that this intimacy in Umr Singh's language is private and secret; it does not break the important public silence. And when Sikandar Khan tries to demonstrate 'how it worked on the Border', Kurban Sahib 'came near to breaking in his head' (pp.14–15), even though he 'privately … said we should have loosed the Sikhs and the Gurkhas on these people till they came in with their foreheads in the dust'.

But although the story half obscures the point, it is his disregard for the Sikh and the Pathan's expertise that brings about his death. They detect the ambush. Not only does he fail to provide covering fire for their retreat, but he turns and *laughs* with heroic insouciance, and is hit, despite Umr Singh's attempts to protect him. The lived ideology of the sahib – his careless daring – runs counter to sense and expediency: it gets him a bullet in the liver. He is – literally – too good for this world.

And his ghost is more effectual than he is – the ghost that puts a stop to the prolonged, palpable and unabashed sadism that Umr Singh indulges in for us. Perhaps what the story is both saying and trying to conceal is that the *ideal* of the sahib, rather than the actuality, is what stands between the British and barbarism. Kurban Sahib is a very dim figure, much paler than the robust Australians. His monument is more concrete than he is, and his epitaph, inscribed in an empty landscape, suggests that he and his kind are a dying breed. Technically, perhaps, the last paragraphs of Kipling's story are flawed. It depends throughout on the illusion of the voice, and then carelessly requires us to *see* the squared up lines and capital letters. But the sense that the sahib is now reduced to *only* this vain and bitter protest is powerful, and reinforced by the last words of the tale: 'Empty, Sahib – all empty!' Is it Umr Singh's heart that is empty, or the ideal? As the privileged citizen of a democracy, Kipling was at liberty to declare what many of his countrymen agreed with: that a popular war had been criminally mishandled. What he was not free to express, and what his story unwittingly half says for him, is that the old ideals, the gamesome English boy and the gentlemanly spirit, are useless.

---

### Race

*2.35* We have already noticed that Umr Singh is depicted as a racist. A classic right-wing response to any charge of racism is an attempt to draw fire to other instances of inter-ethnic hostility, and here it has the effect, at first sight, of making Kipling and his hero seem (dare I say it?) whiter than white. But again, a deeper look reveals that Kipling cannot escape the racism of his class and times. To create an Indian who is so unmistakably a sadist is an act of racism. But sometimes we cannot be sure whether our own times have changed the perspective. When the Sikh and the Pathan share opium after burying the sahib, are we to think of what follows as drug-crazed? Opium is exotic and un-English: a pukka sahib would not use it – though sahibs had turned millions of Chinese into opium addicts to pay for their tea. To us it is criminal, but to the nineteenth century it could be as innocent as aspirin.

*2.36* Though Kurban Sahib calls his bearer 'Father' (thus inverting the more familiar notion of the 'white father' and allowing Kipling to suggest *both* that the sahibs had something to learn from their servants *and* that there was a sentimental intimacy), the real order of command is never in doubt. Yet the sahib depends totally on his servants, both for his basic personal needs (a 'sweeper' – which Umr Singh consents to be – disposes of your excrement), and in warfare. The story pretends there is a buddy-like equality, but what does the Indian get out of it?

2.37   In Kipling's time the 'official' answer would have been *civilization*. It takes a white man's ghost to prevent a 'native' atrocity. (In the next block you will want to compare this with *A Passage to India*: it takes Fielding to persuade Aziz not to prosecute Adela.) This is, of course, appallingly high-handed, but it was the orthodox wisdom and indeed, by the standards of his time, Kipling was the reverse of racist. Just as he had almost singlehandedly transformed the popular image of the common soldier – the arm of imperialism – so he depicted its subject peoples with a new, harsh respect, getting beyond both well-intentioned stereotypes, like that of the Noble Savage, and demeaning ones, of 'natives' as fuzzy-wuzzies round the cannibal pot. Some of the worst stereotyping was found in children's literature, so that young colonial administrators and their memsahibs took up their duties well primed. Kipling did much to change this, and, in the face of popular reductionism, postulated complex, more adult characters in whom he stressed the inevitable difference from any European psyche that resulted from entirely different cultural backgrounds.

2.38   Racism, like sexism, is one of the most deeply naturalized ideologies, and I doubt whether any white should ever dare to assert that a text about blacks is not racist. There are areas of offence to which I am bound to be insensitive, and perhaps, like Kipling, I am most liable to cause offence where I least intend it. And Kipling's text surely is most racist where it least intends to be. It takes for granted, for example, that the friendship of a sahib compensates for subjection. But this friendship needs unpacking. The pairing of the 'straight' Englishman with a roguish, rascally scallywag for a companion, is very familiar and derives from a tradition that goes back to Greek comedy. What's more, Edwardian literature is full of examples of 'manly bonding'. Kurban Sahib has two of these side-kicks and could not function without them. They are in fact a corporate identity, with all the necessary discreditable characteristics portioned off in the 'lesser' half of the team. The Englishman, as I have already suggested, needs the Indian to do his dirty work for him.

2.39   Yet though the Indian represents expedient savagery, he is in the end biddable. The story seems to contradict its title, for it is Umr Singh's war too. The very form says that there is another point of view, and thus it seems potentially subversive. Yet ultimately it reinforces the prevailing imperialist ideology because, by locating the source of the narrative inside Singh's head, it lulls the reader into thinking that no very subversive, rebellious or hostile thoughts about challenging the white master dwell there. The savagery is more problematic. On the one hand it is safely located within the alien (the implication is that no white man would torture for revenge), but on the other hand it is a force hard to control. The ghost has to appear three times before the Sikh and the Pathan are subdued. And this could be taken to suggest the demons that would be let out of the bag if the Indians gained their freedom – with only the ghost of a threadbare ideal to keep them in check.

2.40   Even the act of writing, from this point of view, is an act of colonization. Kipling felt 'authorized' to commandeer the subject race's perspective. And this takes us to a different point. What made Kipling feel entitled to do this was not just a belief in the virtues of British imperialism but a belief that fiction has no frontiers. Though its elliptical, decentred perspective make this in some respects a Modernist tale, Kipling was also a writer in the venerable realist tradition, who believed that whatever his imagination gave him access to, he was entitled to relate. Now we are less sure of this right. Many feminists would argue that as a man cannot fully know what it is like to be a woman, he should not try to write from her point of view. Men have claimed that no woman can create a convincing man. Black people resent being written about by whites, and Theodor Adorno says severely that 'All roles may be played, except that of the worker' (Reader, pp.88–9). So what was intended as an act of imaginative sympathy may unconsciously be an act of appropriation. There will be more on this subject in the next block, where Michael Rossington will be considering the work of Edward Said.

*2.41* 'A Sahibs' War' is a hideously fascinating story that dramatizes the impossible division between the brutality needed to fight and win, and the ineffectual idealism which is useless without it. Adorno, quoting Sartre, says that 'political falsehood stains the aesthetic form'. (Sartre had said that it is impossible to write a good novel in praise of anti-semitism.) Adorno, however, wants to say that *no* political falsehood can be praised in 'good' art. If you have ever suspected that criticism is a kind of intellectual frivolity, you might at least agree that here is an issue of great significance. Does the 'political falsehood' of imperialism 'stain the aesthetic form' of 'A Sahibs' War'? This is not an easy question to answer because, as we have seen, the story's deepest targets are so elusive. We could even argue that the stricture is not broken at all, because on examination it does not really praise or endorse the imperial ethic at all, but only shows that it is an impossibility, built not on ideals but baseness. From what we know of Kipling, this was quite the opposite of his aim. But the less we consider the story to be Kipling's, and the more we think of it and its author as the products of their time and culture, the less relevant moral approval becomes. We may very much dislike certain aspects of the story, but its racism and its cruelty were surely aspects of the political situation which the pressures of writing have forced into the open. Whether intentionally or not, Kipling has revealed the tensions inherent in imperialism, and the silences, the gaps and the contradictions in the story (topics that will be pursued in the next section on Camus) are as crucial as its relatively overt assertions. We should not expect the writer consciously to see his or her times totally objectively or completely. No one can do that. Rather the writing mirrors, in a refracting glass, the writer's complex of conscious and lived ideologies:

> The writer is involved in the movements of his age, but involved in a way which inhibits him from giving a complete account … The writer is not there to articulate the total structure of an epoch; he gives us, rather, an image, a unique and privileged glimpse … The role of the writer, you might say, is to dramatize [*faire vivre*] the historical structure by narrating it … A writer's appeal depends on his conveying a certain knowledge of his age … But this knowledge is not necessarily identical with that of the reader, for the writer's position carries certain rights, notably the right to be in error.
>
> (Macherey, 1978)

# 3  Camus: 'The Outsider'

## ACTIVITY

This section of the block will discuss the theme of 'Literature and ideology' in relation to *L'Etranger* (1942), the novel by Albert Camus (1913–60), in the translation by Joseph Laredo entitled *The Outsider* (1983). Please now read the novel before proceeding any further with the course material. When you have read it, consider the following questions, and make brief notes.

(a)  In what sense, or senses, is Meursault an 'outsider'?

(b)  What explanations does the story provide for the murder of the Arab by Meursault? Did any of these explanations strike you as adequate?

(c)  Do you notice any difference between the narrative techniques of the two parts? In the view of Meursault each presents? In his own view of his situation? And in the language he uses in each part?

(d)  The story ends with Meursault's claim that, even though facing execution, he 'was still happy' (p.117). What is the source of this happiness?

(e)  What is your view of Camus's comments on Meursault printed in the 'Afterword' (pp.118–19)?

Don't forget that in considering these points, you will want to turn back to the text, both to refresh your memory of detail, and to relate such details to the whole story.

---

3.1  Literary study always has to begin from a personal reading of the text. I hope that the questions you've now worked on have helped you to develop your own view of Camus's novel. Before pursuing them further, it will be useful to sketch in some details about Camus's early life and about the situation in which he wrote the novel and a closely related book, *The Myth of Sisyphus*.

3.2  Albert Camus was born in Algiers in November 1913. Algiers was then a French colony which had been acquired by a military conquest begun in 1830, though not completed till about 1860. By Camus's time, Algeria was thought to be finally 'settled', with French rule no longer contested by the indigenous Arab population. Algiers, at first a sort of frontier town, had become a bustling commercial port, the main *entrepôt* for trade between the colony and France, and also with other Mediterranean countries. Governed by a small class of wealthy French colonialists, with a large polyglot European lower-middle and working class (French, Spanish, Italian, Maltese), Algiers was predominantly a European city. But it also had a sizeable Arab population. Camus's father worked for a wine-shipper in Algiers. Called up at the beginning of the 1914–18 War, he fought in its first major battle, when the German advance was halted only a few miles from Paris, dying soon after from severe wounds. His widow moved to Belcourt, a working-class district of Algiers, bringing up her two sons (Albert was the younger), herself working as a house-cleaner and laundress. Camus did well at his primary school and gained a scholarship to the *lycée* where he soon proved an exceptional pupil. Already in his teens he was reading widely (Gide, Montherlant, Malraux), and became determined to be a writer. He also loved sport, particularly football at which he excelled, and swimming. With his friends, he would spend long hours on the Algerian beaches. In 1930, however, he fell ill with tuberculosis, a disease which plagued him for the rest of his life. He attended the University of Algiers from 1933 to 1936, concentrating on philosophy, but his poor health ruled out any career in school-teaching or university lecturing since the authorities demanded a clean bill of health for successful applicants.

3.3   Between 1935 and 1937, he made his living as an actor for a theatrical company he himself founded, *Théatre du Travail*, also directing plays he had either written or adapted from other sources. In 1938, he turned to journalism, working for *Alger-Républicain* which supported the Popular Front against the rising power of Fascism. In 1935, Camus had joined the Communist Party, on whose behalf he disseminated revolutionary propaganda among the Arab population, and organized cultural activities for audiences of trade unionists and other left-wing sympathizers. In 1937, he left the Party, partly because it wouldn't support some Arab nationalists jailed by the French government. As a journalist for *Alger-Républicain*, he continued to campaign against the unjust treatment of the Arab population of Algiers. A few months after the outbreak of the 1939–45 War, *Alger-Républicain* was closed down because of its anti-war policies and, needing another job, Camus went to Paris where again he worked as a journalist. Here, he completed *The Outsider* which he had been working on since 1938. During this period he was also writing the book that became *The Myth of Sisyphus*, and a play, *Caligula*. Following the German victory over France in June 1940, he moved to Lyon, and then back to Algeria where he revised *The Outsider*. With the help of French acquaintances, it was accepted for publication by the Paris publishing firm Gallimard, which brought it out in June 1942. Gallimard also accepted *The Myth of Sisyphus*, but on account of German censorship had to delete a chapter about Kafka, who was Jewish. The book appeared in December 1942. During 1942, however, Camus's tubercular condition obliged him to move back to France to a village in the Massif Central, and a year later to Paris. He had meanwhile joined the French Resistance movement and was writing for *Combat*, its newspaper, articles and editorials which, when their authorship was disclosed after the war, made him famous. Meanwhile, both *The Outsider* and *The Myth of Sisyphus* were well received in French intellectual circles. Outlining the historical contexts which contributed to the novel's success, Patrick McCarthy has written:

> A historical contradiction is involved because the novel, which springs from pre-war Algeria, was read during the dreary days of the [German] Occupation … it was Camus's working-class and Algerian background which led him to the themes that struck a chord in the Paris of 1942, namely, the illegitimacy of authority and the primacy of concrete, individual experience. Yet the specifically Algerian features – the depiction of the pied-noir hero and the Arab problem – were generally overlooked, while [the novel] was read in a supposedly universal but in fact Western European context, as a manual of how an individual may live in a world without authentic values.
>
> (McCarthy, 1988, p.14; *pied-noir* was the colloquial term for the French-Algerian working class to which Meursault and his friends belong)

## SAMPLE ANSWERS

To return to the questions listed at the beginning of this section here are my sample answers.

(a)   Meursault is an 'outsider' in the sense that he is detached from the attitudes and behaviour that his society considers appropriate and, further, he seems not to care. He doesn't weep at his mother's funeral. He is glad to get back to his own life. The day after the funeral he enjoys himself swimming, takes Marie to a comic film in the evening, and they spend the night together. He's not ambitious in his work, doesn't want 'to get on'. When Marie asks him if he loves her, he says it's a meaningless question. Asked by his lawyer about his feelings over his mother's death, he says that most people at one time or another wish for the death of people they love. Asked by the examining magistrate whether he felt regret for the murder of the Arab, he says only 'a kind of annoyance' (p.69). In these and other ways, he concedes not an inch to the demand of society that he feel and act in a socially-approved way. He remains an alien, then, in a fundamental sense, one whose refusal to conform to the approved rituals, customs and beliefs of his society sets him outside it, and so he is perceived by it as potentially subversive.

(b)  The prosecutor claims that Meursault, having fired one shot, then after a pause, four more, acted out of murderous deliberation. Meursault's friend Celeste says 'it was a mishap' (p.89). The defence lawyer says the Arab had provoked Meursault. Meursault says it was the heat and glare of the sun that prompted him to shoot. Earlier, when the examining magistrate presses the question about firing five shots, four at a dead body, Meursault simply doesn't answer, not even to say 'I don't know'. I find I can accept none of these accounts as adequately explaining Meursault's act. The story seems to me to leave it unexplained, an enigma (though perhaps 'mishap' comes nearest).

(c)  The difference between the two parts which I find most striking lies in their character as narratives. In the first, there is no strong narrative movement. The succession of events is casual, moving in no direction that we can begin to guess. Using the terminology for narrative analysis introduced in Block 1, it is not easy to distinguish between 'kernels' (events crucial to advancing the story) and 'satellites' (events not crucial in that way, but describing scenes, analysing character, providing atmosphere, etc.). Here is a representative paragraph from Part One:

> I turned my chair round like the tobacconist's because I found it more comfortable that way. I smoked a couple of cigarettes, went inside to get some chocolate and came back to the window to eat it. Soon after that, the sky clouded over and I thought we were going to have a summer storm. It gradually cleared again though. But the passing clouds had left a sort of threat of rain hanging over the street which made it more gloomy. I watched the sky for a long time.
>
> (p.26)

Taking the paragraph as a whole, the only series of 'kernels' it belongs to is provided by preceding and succeeding paragraphs which register little more than the slow passage of time. Thus, the next one begins: 'At five o'clock there was a lot of noise as some trams arrived'; followed by the next: 'The day advanced a bit more'; then, 'the street lamps suddenly came on… ' (pp.26–7). Within the paragraph the events also detail the passing hours, but primarily they function as 'satellites', building up our sense of Meursault's character, uninvolved, passive, mildly hedonistic, as well as filling in details about the city and the climate. This narrative technique is characteristic of Part One, and accounts for its apparently desultory movement. When in Part Two the prosecutor chooses to represent the events of Part One as adding up to a 'plot', in which Meursault has teamed up with Raymond in order to punish the Moorish girl, and then take revenge on Raymond's behalf on the Arab who'd wounded him, we know that this 'plot' is pure invention. The Part One narrative has presented these and other events as merely *happening to* Meursault, who is acted upon, rather than acting, living without long-term purposes or aims, minute by minute, absorbed in his immediate sensations and feelings of pleasure or discomfort. So the climax of Part One is surely a total surprise? There seems no reason why, after the fight and the return to the beach-house, Meursault doesn't join his friends indoors, out of the sun, choosing instead to walk back along the shore despite the intense heat. We get no sense that a murder is imminent. Even here Meursault seems to drift from event to event, aimlessly.

Part Two, by contrast, has a stronger narrative 'drive' mainly provided by the trial and our concern about whether Meursault will be judged guilty or not. We know *this* story will arrive at one of two conclusions: innocent or guilty, life or death. Though it has also to be said of Part Two that Meursault's apparent indifference to the outcome sheds a dream-like quality on the events, as if they were happening to someone else. Only in the last pages does Meursault begin to reveal conviction and purpose. There is the further point that since Part Two recapitulates many of the events of Part One we begin to sense that, after all, these events had been subjected to skilful narrative shaping by the writer. We realize that the opening pages especially (Meursault's visit to the home, the funeral, how he behaves on his return) are as they are in order to support – or at least not to contradict – the Part Two interpretation of Meursault as a callous and unfeeling criminal. You'll remember that the trial scenes make far more of Meursault's allegedly unfilial behaviour than of the Arab's death. So, the contrast between the seemingly casual succession of events in Part One and the more purposive narrative of Part Two is deliberate. On the one hand, a life; on the other, interpretations of that life: the examining magistrate's, the prosecutor's, the judge's, the priest's, and in the last pages, Meursault's, each investing it with a different meaning and purpose.

As to other differences, the Meursault of Part Two is more reflective than his predecessor, not surprisingly. In Part One, it is not that we are presented with an unthinking Meursault, so much as one whose train of thought is never explicit. For example, in the mortuary, having drunk a cup of coffee, he tells us:

I then wanted a cigarette. But I hesitated because I didn't know if I could smoke in front of mother. I thought it over, it really didn't matter.

(p.14)

We don't hear the full argument, but this is an early example of the laconic independence of thought which will be turned against him at the trial. Again, after their swim, when Marie notices he has on a black tie and hears the reason:

She recoiled slightly, but made no remark. I felt like telling her it wasn't my fault, but I stopped myself because I remembered that I'd already said that to my boss. It didn't mean anything. In any case, you're always partly to blame.

(p.24)

Notice that last sentence. It qualifies, doesn't it, what could seem mere indifference? 'It didn't mean anything' dismisses the point of the conventional black tie and of Marie's slightly shocked response; it is Meursault's comment on that response. But the addition 'you're always partly to blame' both shows that he understands the conventional feeling he has offended, and by himself accepting blame, concedes it some validity. The gap between the sentences points to unspoken thought of some complexity.

Still, on the whole, the Meursault of Part One exists for us primarily in terms of his sensations and feelings, what he sees, hears and feels, what gives him pleasure, or boredom, or unease. Whereas in Part Two, his ideas are more explicit: about the examining magistrate, the prison routine, the trial, and the priest. In Part One, the reader is primarily invited to *observe* Meursault's life, but in Part Two becomes sympathetically involved with his fate. The novel uses Meursault's wondering detachment from the court proceedings to show up their manifest injustice, the rhetorical antics of the prosecuting counsel, the sense in which someone other than the Meursault we've become familiar with in Part One, seems to be on trial, as indeed he himself remarks. Or again, in the prison, Meursault's uncomplaining account (for example, of the conditions under which prisoners are allowed to speak to relatives and friends), without adding up to an *overt* attack on the prison system, brings home to us its inhumane rigour, and linked to the judicial process which requires this system, reminds us that all the prisoners, like Meursault, are 'dehumanized' by it.

Meursault's own view of his situation also changes. In Part One, we hardly know *how* he views his life or the world in which he lives, whereas in Part Two, he begins to reflect and judge, a process culminating in his violent rebuff of the priest's attempted consolations. The language of the two parts differs accordingly. Part One is descriptive, concrete, full of colour and feeling, each episode concentrating on the sensory world congenial to Meursault's consciousness. Part Two is more reflective, more discerning, not lacking in concrete detail, but since Meursault is now imprisoned, cut off from normal living, less vividly registered.

(d) Meursault's final claim to be 'still happy': how did you account for this? After all, he tells us at the end of Part One that the death of the Arab had meant the beginning of 'unhappiness', which is to say, the end of the kind of life Meursault had been living. The reason lies in the way he rejects the priest's Christian view of life:

…I was sure of myself, sure of everything, surer than he was, sure of my life and sure of the death that was coming to me. Yes, that was all I had. But at least it was a truth which I had hold of just as it had hold of me. I'd been right, I was still right, I was always right.

(p.115)

Right in what way? In his belief that there is only this life, that death ends it all for *everybody*, and to live at all is in itself enough. The certain fact of death means that it doesn't matter how, or when, or for what reason, we actually die. Grasping this basic truth, Meursault,

looked up at the mass of signs and stars in the night sky and laid myself open for the first time to the benign indifference of the world.

(p.117)

By 'indifference' he means that the material world cares nothing for human pain or for human desire for a life beyond death. He is now 'happy' because he accepts this irrefutable truth.

(e) Camus's own account of Meursault commends him for resolving 'without any heroic pretensions … to die for the truth' (p.119). The truth Meursault dies for, or at least discovers shortly before he dies, is the source of his final happiness. There is only this life. And for this reason any metaphysical, religious and moral system in whose terms we might judge this or that way of living superior, are illusions. Meursault is a sort of secular Christ (Camus claims), executed not for the murder, but because he refuses to concede the validity of the false values enforced by society. What did you make of this? Can it be reconciled with the fact that Meursault killed the Arab? Is Camus providing a decisive authorial account of the killing, i.e. that it *wasn't* murder, but a 'mishap', and in any case, of no importance beside the fact that Meursault was judged guilty on the irrelevant ground that he hadn't wept at his mother's funeral?

3.4   What authors say about their work is always interesting, but can it settle uncertainties and problems generated by the work itself? There is here both a particular issue about the novel, and a general issue about the status of Camus's subsequent authorial comment, to which we will have to return.

## ACTIVITY

Let's now move to the theme of the block, *Literature and Ideology*, in its relation to Camus's novel. Taking 'ideology' in its simplest sense, does *The Outsider* urge a point of view on the reader? As we've seen, Meursault claims that his view of life is 'right' (p.115), but does the novel support him? Do we, as readers, agree that he has successfully overthrown the validity, both of the legal system that condemns him to death, and of the Christian beliefs passionately held by the examining magistrates and the priest? In considering this, don't forget Camus's 'Afterword'.

## DISCUSSION

Here are two views of the question.

(a)   The whole structure and momentum of the novel builds towards Meursault's final statements. The seemingly casual organization of Part One followed by the trial in Part Two puts the reader on Meursault's side, destroys the moral and legal authority claimed by the court, of the State for which the court speaks, and of the Christian beliefs to which the magistrate and priest appeal as their ultimate sanction. The novel shows Meursault finally articulating the principles by which he has lived, and it presents them to the reader as 'right'. Camus's description of Meursault as 'the only Christ that we deserve' confirms this reading. It amounts to an unqualified endorsement of his views. The novel thus offers an express and unambiguous 'ideological' message, whose vehicle is the life and final utterance of Meursault.

(b)   Meursault's trial was a farcical disgrace; that he should be executed because he didn't weep at his mother's funeral is a scandalous indictment of a deeply-flawed and inhumane judicial system; that he should angrily reject a religion complicit with such a system is entirely understandable; and that he should think as he finally does commands our admiration for its stoical courage. Nevertheless, as readers, we are not asked to agree with Meursault's opinions. The novel as a whole offers no sustained arguments on his behalf. The priest's beliefs, sincerely and sympathetically expressed, stand in unresolved opposition to Meursault's; while Camus's phrase, in identifying Meursault with Christ – both virtuous and heroic victims of the State – points to a complex attitude towards Christianity rather than a blunt rejection. We sympathize with Meursault, but not uncritically: he did kill the Arab, and is remarkably unconcerned about his deed. Far from proposing an explicit philosophical message, the novel sets out for our sympathetic, but also detached, contemplation Meursault's state of mind and feeling as the tragic conclusion to a particular human life.

Which view do you take? And why? Having made your choice, consider further whether these are the only possibilities. Do these summaries omit important aspects? I'll postpone offering my own comment till we've brought into the discussion Camus's explicit philosophical ideas as set out in *The Myth of Sisyphus*.

## The myth of Sisyphus

3.5   From the details about Camus's life and writings given in paragraphs 3.2–3, we've seen that *The Myth of Sisyphus* was written during the same period that he was writing the novel. In fact, it represents his explicit philosophical thinking in those years. Here is how he described the book in a preface for the first (1955) edition:

> The fundamental subject of *The Myth of Sisyphus* is this: it is legitimate and necessary to wonder whether life has a meaning; therefore it is legitimate to meet the problem of suicide face to face. The answer, underlying and appearing through the paradoxes which cover it, is this: even if one does not believe in God, suicide is not legitimate. Written fifteen years ago, in 1940, amidst the French and European disaster, this book declares that even within the limits of nihilism, it is possible to find the means to proceed beyond nihilism. ...Although *The Myth of Sisyphus* poses mortal problems, it sums itself up for me as a lucid invitation to live and create, in the very midst of the desert.
>
> (Camus, 1975, p.7)

The book itself opens with a paragraph that has become famous:

> There is but one truly serious philosophical problem and that is suicide. Judging whether life is or is not worth living amounts to answering the fundamental question of philosophy. All the rest – whether or not the world has three dimensions, whether the mind has nine or twelve categories – comes afterwards. And if it is true, as Nietzsche claims, that a philosopher, to deserve our respect, must preach by example, you can appreciate the importance of that reply, for it will precede the definitive act. These are facts the heart can feel; yet they call for careful study before they become clear to the intellect.
>
> (Ibid., p.11)

3.6   Camus then proceeds to illustrate what he calls life's radical 'absurdity', by which he means something stronger than 'stupidity'. (In French, *absurde* means *contraire à la raison*; 'senseless' is perhaps the nearest English equivalent.) He starts from the position that the human desire that life should 'make sense' cannot be satisfied:

> This world in itself is not reasonable, that is all that can be said. But what is absurd is the confrontation of the irrational and the wild longing for clarity whose call echoes in the human heart. The absurd depends as much on man as on the world. For the moment it is all that links them together. It binds them one to the other as only hatred can weld two creatures together. This is all I can discern clearly in this measureless universe where my adventure takes place.
>
> (Ibid., p.26)

He assumes that the Christian answer to this predicament is untenable. There is no supernatural deity upon whose wisely mysterious dispensations, transcending the limits of human reason, religious conviction can repose. There is no after-life to compensate for the bleak frustrations, casual sufferings and irreversible injustices, which make up the average human lot. There is the material universe whose impersonal structures and blind procedures take no account of human consciousness. There is also the history of human behaviour, century upon century, before which the seeker after justifying explanations can only retire in bafflement and despair. Finally, there is human mortality, the inescapable fate which calls into question the lasting value of every human achievement. Human life is 'absurd', not because it yields no meaning, but because, yielding no meaning, human beings nevertheless passionately seek one.

3.7   Camus then discusses a number of philosophers (Kierkegaard, Chestov, Heidegger, Jaspers, Husserl) who also concede that life negates 'human reason' (p.43). The details of this argument we don't need to pursue here, but Camus's objections come down to this: such philosophers refuse equal recognition to *both* terms of the conflict – the desire that life satisfy human reason, and its negation of that desire. For Camus, both these terms, with the irreconcilable conflict between them, constitute the truth of the human condition. He proposes a philosophy of living *'without appeal'* (p.53), which accepts the radical contradiction of 'the absurd', denying itself the illusion of hope (for an after-life) and of nostalgia (melancholic longing for a rational solution). To be mature, for Camus, is to live the contradiction in full consciousness, with courage and – paradoxical though it may seem – with stoical joy; and moreover, to live the contradiction every day, since on every day death may come. That is his case against the view that suicide is the logical answer to the meaninglessness of life. Suicide amounts to throwing in the towel, and philosophies that resolve 'absurdity' by appealing to metaphysics or mysticism are no different. They amount to 'philosophical suicide' (p.43), because while they accept that life is without meaning, they refuse to honour the human passion that it shouldn't be.

3.8   In thus summarizing Camus's argument, there is a danger of misrepresentation. *The Myth of Sisyphus* is a strikingly personal book, and as 'philosophy' I suspect that professional philosophers would describe it as 'literary', doubtless in mild disparagement. As well as philosophers, Camus draws on many other novelists (Dostoevsky, Proust, Kafka), and he quotes with approval Nietzsche's apothegm:

> 'Art and nothing but art; we have art in order not to die of the truth.'
>
> (p.86)

It is also 'literary' in its individually expressive style.

## ACTIVITY

Before returning to the relationship of *The Myth of Sisyphus* to *The Outsider*, read through these extracts which convey better than my summary argument the kind of book it is:

> Suicide has never been dealt with except as a social phenomenon. ...we are concerned here, at the outset, with the relationship between individual thought and suicide. An act like this is prepared within the silence of the heart, as is a great work of art. The man himself is ignorant of it. One evening he pulls the trigger or jumps. Of an apartment-building manager who had killed himself I was told that he had lost his daughter five years before, that he had changed greatly since and that that experience had 'undermined' him. A more exact word cannot be imagined. Beginning to think is beginning to be undermined.
>
> (Ibid., p.12)

> We get into the habit of living before acquiring the habit of thinking.
>
> (Ibid., p.15)

At the heart of all beauty lies something inhuman, and these hills, the softness of the sky, the outline of these trees at this very minute lose the illusory meaning with which we had clothed them, henceforth more remote than a lost paradise. The primitive hostility of the world rises up to face us across millenia. ...The world evades us because it becomes itself again. That stage-scenery masked by habit becomes again what it is. It withdraws at a distance from us. Just as there are days when, under the familiar face of a woman, we see as a stranger her we had loved months or years ago, perhaps we shall come even to desire what suddenly leaves us alone. But the time has not yet come. Just one thing: that denseness and that strangeness of the world is the absurd.

(Ibid., p.20)

The mind's deepest desire, even in its most elaborate operations, parallels man's unconscious feelings in the face of his universe: it is an insistence upon familiarity, an appetite for clarity. Understanding the world for a man is reducing it to the human, stamping it with his seal. The cat's universe is not the universe of the ant-hill.

(Ibid., pp.22–3)

And here are trees and I know their gnarled surface, water and I feel its taste. These scents of grass and stars at night, certain evenings when the heart relaxes – how shall I negate this world whose power and strength I feel? Yet all the knowledge on earth will give me nothing to assure me that this world is mine. You describe it to me and you teach me to classify it. You enumerate its laws and in my thirst for knowledge I admit that they are true. You take apart its mechanism and my hope increases. At the final stage you teach me that this wondrous and multi-coloured universe can be reduced to the atom and that the atom itself can be reduced to the electron. All this is good and I wait for you to continue. But you tell me of an invisible planetary system in which electrons gravitate round a nucleus. You explain this world to me with an image. I realize then that you have been reduced to poetry: I shall never know. Have I the time to become indignant?

(Ibid., pp.24–5)

The contrary of suicide, in fact, is the man condemned to death.

(Ibid., p.54)

The gods had condemned Sisyphus to ceaselessly rolling a rock to the top of a mountain, whence the stone would fall back of its own weight. They had thought with some reason that there is no more dreadful punishment than futile and hopeless labour. ...Sisyphus, proletarian of the gods, powerless and rebellious, knows the whole extent of his wretched condition; it is what he thinks of during his descent. The lucidity that was to constitute his torture at the same time crowns his victory. There is no fate that cannot be surmounted by scorn.

I leave Sisyphus at the foot of the mountain! One always finds one's burden again. But Sisyphus teaches the higher fidelity that negates the gods and raises rocks. The universe henceforth without a master seems to him neither sterile nor futile. Each atom of that stone, each mineral flake of that night-filled mountain, in itself forms a world. The struggle itself towards the heights is enough to fill a man's heart. One must imagine Sisyphus happy.

(Ibid., pp.107–11)

## ACTIVITY

How far, then, is the philosophy argued for in *The Myth of Sisyphus* recommended in *The Outsider*? How far can it be said to represent the 'ideology' of the novel, the point of view of whose truth the novel seeks to persuade us?

## SAMPLE ANSWER

Here are some sentences from Meursault's last words, his answer to the chaplain:

> I'd lived in a certain way and I could just as well have lived in a different way. I'd done this and I hadn't done that. I hadn't done one thing whereas I had done another. So what? It was as if I'd been waiting all along for this very moment and for the early dawn when I'd be justified. Nothing, nothing mattered and I knew very well why. He too knew why. From the depths of my future, throughout the whole of this absurd life I'd been leading, I'd felt a vague breath drifting toward me across all the years that were still to come ... What did other people's deaths or a mother's love matter to me, what did his God or the lives people chose or the destinies they selected matter to me, when one and the same destiny was to select me and thousands of millions of other privileged people who, like him, called themselves my brothers. Didn't he understand? Everyone was privileged. There were only privileged people. The others too would be condemned one day. He too would be condemned.
>
> (pp.115–16)

Meursault is not a philosopher, nor like Camus a novelist widely read in philosophy, but here surely is his way of formulating the position elaborated in *The Myth of Sisyphus*. The explicit clue, if one is needed, lies in the phrase 'the whole of this absurd life I'd been leading'. And, facing his execution, he goes on to say:

> I looked up at the mass of signs and stars in the night sky and laid myself open for the first time to the benign indifference of the world. And finding it so much like myself, in fact so fraternal, I realized that I'd been happy, and that I was still happy.
>
> (p.117)

This final affirmation is 'Sisyphean'. Happiness is only possible when the world's 'indifference' to human beings, once accepted, becomes 'benign' rather than the standing offence to reason with which philosophers vainly struggle. But given the connection, does this also mean that we have identified the novel's 'ideology'? This is a question to be discussed, rather than simply answered.

## DISCUSSION

We've seen that, structurally, the novel builds towards these closing speeches by Meursault, and also that Camus later endorsed the notion of Meursault as an heroic truth-teller and innocent victim of the ideological falsities of Church and State. Going back to the sample answers offered on pages 30–31, if you opted for the first, you would have to agree that, yes, Camus's 'Afterword' fairly indicates the novel's 'ideology', and that further reference to *The Myth of Sisyphus* supports him. If you opted for the second, you would be resisting this simplest conception of 'ideology' – that novels resemble envelopes from which the reader extracts a definite point of view – but nevertheless agreeing that without directly urging the philosophy of 'the absurd' upon the reader, it represents it in a most sympathetic light.

3.9 That would be my choice, except for the further possibility that the novel also raises issues not accounted for by either alternative. In considering these, we can begin by recalling the more complex notion of 'ideology' as implicit 'world-view', to use the term of Georg Lukács introduced in Block 2 Section 8, which directs our attention not to the *explicit* ideology represented in Meursault's life and opinions, but to other less visible assumptions embedded in the novel's structure.

*3.10* Lukács argued that Modernist texts conveyed a fundamental assertion about the human condition, that it was solitary, apolitical, and ahistorical. His own Marxist position required him to criticize this since, for the Marxist, such a view must mean a withdrawal from 'reality' which is always and inescapably historical, and therefore can only be adequately rendered within social, political and economic perspectives. Pierre Macherey, also a Marxist, shared the same conviction but he offered a different view of the relationship between literary texts and the historical reality which shaped their development. For Lukács, literary texts directly, even if only by implication, express a relatively homogeneous ideology, which 'reflects' the social and cultural position of their writers. Thus, the ideologies of *The Waste Land* or *Mrs Dalloway* are direct fictional embodiments of ideas which their writers can be shown to hold in their discursive essays, or in the works of other writers they admire. But Macherey rejects this 'reflectionist' argument. For him, literary texts incorporate ideological positions, including whatever happens to be the writer's particular point of view, but in such a way as to show them up for illusions. Macherey conceives of the writer, not as a creator expressing a personal 'vision', but as a *labourer*, who constructs fictions from the material his society makes available: literary genres and conventions, social practices, ways of speaking and behaving, institutional structures, contemporary beliefs and attitudes, and especially the large-scale ideological systems within which people make sense of their lives. In pre-socialist society such systems are always, from the Marxist angle, 'false consciousness', which is not to say they are crude lies and deceptions put about in the interests of the ruling class. Thus, in the Middle Ages, feudal aristocratic conceptions of honour and duty amounted to a 'false consciousness', yet were nevertheless essential in sustaining and validating the social and economic position of the land-owning class, and as such sincerely held to be true by that class and by those they ruled. 'Ideology' in this sense, when incorporated into literary texts, so Macherey argues, undergoes a transformation. Instead of 'reflecting' it, the texts bring into view its internal contradictions, its inability to provide a coherent account of the fictional situations elaborated in the text. Far from providing a homogeneous world-view, which can be replicated outside the text, the fiction reveals inexplicable gaps and omissions, conflicts, and significant silences on major issues, which speak more eloquently than its overt commentary.

## Macherey: *A Theory of Literary Production*

*ACTIVITY*

The extracts from Macherey's *A Theory of Literary Production* in the Reader propose this idea (pp.215–22). Please read them now. Though they are not at all jargon-ridden, you will probably find the tight argument demanding. It may help you to concentrate on such questions as:

(a)  How does Macherey define the task of the literary critic and how does he distinguish it from the familiar notions of 'interpretation' and 'evaluation'?

(b)  How does he conceive of the relationship between what a text says overtly, and what it doesn't – between its 'speech' and its 'silence'?

*SAMPLE ANSWERS*

(a)  The text 'does not *know* itself' (p.216). The critic's task is not to explicate, to unfold, what the text incompletely says, a process which amounts to completing the text with an interpretative commentary. What the critic should undertake is a description of the knowledge which the text unknowingly contains. This knowledge is peculiar to the text, and not to be judged by an external criterion (such as Lukács invokes when he criticizes Modernist texts for their failure to render the full social reality of their times). The critic is therefore not a judge or evaluator. His task is more like that of a scientist describing the structure of a natural object.

(b)  What a text says (its speech) is related to what it doesn't (its silence) in a manner analogous to the relationship between the Freudian notions of 'conscious' and 'unconscious'. A text is 'implicit' not in those aspects where the writer has consciously chosen to be laconic or enigmatic, but in the *unspoken* element which is the necessary sub-structure for what is 'explicit'. The critic's task is to point out this relationship, as a Freudian psychoanalyst would point to the censored material of which the account of a dream is the conscious speech. Macherey stresses that this is nothing to do with analysing *the writer*, as is the practice of psycho-biographers. The text itself reveals both 'conscious' and necessarily 'unconscious' components. The knowledge it offers resides in each and in the relation between them. The 'speech' of a text is what it can say, its 'silence' what it cannot say, and what it can say is a direct product of what it cannot say.

*3.11*  What is the advantage of this more difficult and complicated account of 'the ideology of the text'? I would suggest two points. First, unlike the Lukacsian view, which in this respect resembles non-Marxist socio-political commentary on literary texts, it is not 'reductionist'. It respects the specificity of texts, as Macherey claims, and this is surely a cardinal issue for any reader of literature. Put in its simplest terms, the *way* a novel, poem or play says what it says, cannot be reproduced in discursive language. Macherey's argument accepts this. Second, he offers a more satisfactory account of the relationship between the text and the non-textual world. Far from reproducing their non-textual sources, which include 'ideologies', the text reformulates this material, and so provides a kind of knowledge of the non-textual world, not otherwise available. This implicitly allots a high general valuation to literary texts, even if in detail the Machereyan critic refuses the traditional role of judge and evaluator. What remains uncertain, however, is whether all texts, and not just those already highly-regarded, are equally worth attention. There is also the tricky question of distinguishing the 'unconscious' elements in a text from those elisions and compressions of topics or issues which the writer has deliberately chosen not to spell out.

*ACTIVITY*

However, bearing Macherey's account in mind, let us return to *The Outsider*. If the 'speech' of the novel primarily resides in the way Meursault's life and death represent 'absurdist' philosophy, is there also a 'silence' composed of omissions, gaps, failures to open up key issues which the reader, alerted by Macherey's ideas, can identify? Before making up your mind about this, read over my comments in paragraphs 3.9–3.10.

## DISCUSSION

My own view is that there is a 'silence' in *The Outsider*, about a major issue which the story touches on and then leaves unexplained: why Meursault shot the Arab five times. The prosecutor cites this as evidence of Meursault's unfeeling ruthlessness, already indicated by cold indifference to his mother's death. But we know this is merely a legal performance. The real problem to my mind is that Meursault, given the chance to explain his action by the examining magistrate, has no answer:

> ... the magistrate then asked me if I'd fired all five shots at once. I thought it over and specified that I'd only fired once to start with and then, a few seconds later, the other four shots. 'Why did you pause between the first and the second shot?' he said. Once again I saw the red beach in front of me and felt the burning sun on my forehead. But this time I didn't answer. Throughout the silence which followed, the magistrate looked flustered. He sat down, ran his fingers through his hair, put his elbows on his desk and leaned slightly towards me with a strange expression on his face. 'Why, why did you fire at a dead body?' Once again I didn't know what to answer. The magistrate wiped his hands across his forehead and repeated his question in a slightly broken voice, 'Why? You must tell me. Why?' I still didn't say anything.
>
> (p.67)

The narrative dwells on the issue, yet finally leaves it unexplained. Was it the sun and the heat? Possibly. But as the magistrate brings out, the pause between the first and second shots implies deliberation. Moreover, if Meursault 'didn't know what to answer', why doesn't he say so? What could be simpler? If, as his friend Celeste later says, 'it was a mishap' (p.89), and if at the same time we reject the prosecutor's explanation, why does the scene with the examining magistrate leave the reader (this reader, at any rate) with the sense that even if the shooting started as an accident caused by the heat, it turned into something quite different which the narrative never discloses?

In what respect does this raise a *major* issue? Might it not be a mere detail, a loose end, about which it's pointless to make a fuss? Let me suggest some reasons. We've seen that *The Outsider* is subtly planned. The narrative technique of Part One, seemingly desultory and episodic, is intended to provide significant contrast with Part Two. Such a scheme persuades me to take all the detail seriously, and especially this one, since the narrative dwells on it. Then, there is the fact that, as an issue, the actual murder disappears from view in Part Two. All the attention is on the legal process whereby Meursault is judged guilty. Not that Meursault denies his guilt, or protests against his punishment. Replying to the priest who tries to convince him that he should confess to having sinned, he only says:

> ... I didn't know what a sin was. I'd simply been told that I was guilty. I was guilty and I was paying for it and there was nothing more that could be asked of me.
>
> (p.113)

Here, the *fact* of the murder has been displaced by the ideological debate between Christian priest and 'absurdist' hero. And this is characteristic of Meursault in Part Two where he hardly seems to recognize that, after all, for no particular reason he did indeed shoot the Arab. Then consider from Part One his own account of the shooting:

> The trigger gave, I felt the underside of the polished butt and it was there, in that sharp but deafening noise, that it all started. I shook off the sweat and the sun. I realized that I'd destroyed the balance of the day and the perfect silence of this beach where I'd been happy. And I fired four more times at a lifeless body and the bullets sank in without leaving a mark. And it was like giving four sharp knocks at the door of unhappiness.
>
> (p.60)

Well, yes, he has destroyed his own happiness, but does he realize he's rather more thoroughly destroyed someone else's? Remember that these questions are being pressed not at all *to mount a criticism of Meursault*, but to point to the novel's 'silence' about issues which its detailed account nevertheless prompts us to raise.

There is also 'silence' of a literal kind. The victim never speaks, nor does he have a name. Once he is called 'Raymond's Arab' (p.58), otherwise he is simply 'the Arab', while his companion is equally anonymous. Raymond's 'Moorish' girl doesn't have a name either (p.36). On one of the few occasions when, in Part One, the Arab population of Algiers is mentioned, Meursault reports:

> They were looking at us in silence, but in their own special way, as if we were nothing more than blocks of stone or dead trees.
>
> (p.50)

Do we not have to remind ourselves that the fight on the beach had, from the point of view of the Arabs, a specific cause? The girl whom Raymond beats up is the sister of the Arab who wounds Raymond, and is then shot by Meursault. The one representation of Arabs which accords them something approaching a human identity occurs in the prison scene (pp. 71–4), but here the issue is that, like Meursault, they are victims of a legal system about to be shown as profoundly unjust. Once the trial begins 'the Arab' is forgotten.

## ACTIVITY

Macherey argued for a *connection* between the 'speech' of a novel and its 'silence'. How does this apply to *The Outsider*? You need to recall here a point about the novel's historical context (see the outline at the beginning of this section), and also that Algeria was, in Camus's time, a French colony where an indigenous Arab population had been brought into subjection. Macherey also directs our attention to the way a novel can reveal contradictions within the ideology it incorporates. What contradictions does *The Outsider* reveal?

## DISCUSSION

The connection between the novel's 'speech' (the overt ideological conflict between Absurdist philosophy and the French judicial practice with which Christianity is held to be complicit) and its 'silence' (the anonymity of the murdered Arab, the far greater condemnatory weight laid upon Meursault's indifference to his mother's death) lies in the evident colonialist bias of the judicial system. The court claims to administer *justice*, fearlessly and objectively: Meursault is to be executed 'in the name of the French people' (p.103). But in order to make its case it skews the argument from the major to a minor issue, as if the killing of an Arab is in itself an insufficient offence. The 'speech' of the novel, which aims to demolish the court's moral authority, can only do so by forgetting what Meursault actually did. It is in this sense that the novel doesn't 'know itself'. What it doesn't know (its 'silence') is nevertheless enough to query the generalizing impartiality of the philosophical debate. It shows up not only the contradiction within the ideology of French justice, but also a blind spot in Meursault's Absurdist ideology. Meursault triumphs over the priest by claiming that since mortality is a general human fate, 'everyone was privileged' (life itself being the privilege) and everyone, the priest included, 'would be condemned one day', would die (p.116). What this argument ignores – indeed seems to have no place for – is the difference between dying and being murdered.

*3.12* This aspect of *The Outsider*, as Patrick McCarthy's comment indicates (see paragraph 3.3), at first attracted no attention. But the Algerian struggle for independence from France during the 1950s, which obliged Camus to state his position as a reluctant supporter of the French cause, and in subsequent years the impact of anti-imperialist struggles in many countries, prompted commentators on Camus's work to take notice of the colonialist issue, both in *The Outsider* and in other novels. Conor Cruise O'Brien, to whom the above discussion owes much, considered Meursault and Camus as both unaware of and indifferent to the novel's 'racist' implications. His book on Camus in the Fontana Modern Masters series appeared in 1970. Philip Thody's *Albert Camus* (1961), in striking contrast, concentrated on the novel's philosophical argument, proposing that Meursault, far from arriving at his final affirmation as a consequence of what has happened, was in full possession of these ideas from the beginning. Brian Masters rejects the O'Brien position as a 'searing irrelevance' produced by 'one who views the world through permanently fixed political spectacles' (1974, p.33). McCarthy, however, complements O'Brien's 'political' interpretation with a psychoanalytical approach to Meursault's relationship with his mother.

*3.13* The argument I have concentrated on here, however, is the way in which Macherey's account of 'the ideology of the text' points to *The Outsider*'s internal contradictoriness, the way in which its overt ideological debate is undermined by the fictional situations which give rise to that debate. This seems to me a better way to consider the colonialist issue, because it avoids necessarily inconclusive debates about Meursault's consciousness, as also about Camus's when he wrote the novel. Or rather, it insists that the novel as a whole is the fullest evidence we have of Camus's consciousness, and if this evidence points to contradictions which his later comment on *The Outsider* fails to recognize, that should not surprise us. Authorial comments on a text are not privileged.

*3.14* Finally, to summarize the main points about Macherey's argument in respect of the block theme:

(a) literary texts incorporate ideologies from the non-textual world;

(b) literary texts do not 'reflect' such ideologies, but re-present them in a different form;

(c) this re-presentation reveals their internal inconsistencies, their inability to provide a satisfactory account of the fictional situations provided by the text;

(d) the text thus provides an implicit critique which undermines their claim to authority.

# 4 Althusser, Freud and feminism

*4.1*  The following 'debate' section builds on some of the ideas put forward in Section 1, attempts to develop them and to indicate some possible common ground between recent Marxist theories and other important areas where ideological and literary concerns coincide. The Reader text for this section is an extract from Lionel Trilling, *The Liberal Imagination*.

*4.2*  You were introduced to the French neo-Marxist philosopher Louis Althusser in Section 1, at the end of the Terry Eagleton reading. We need to divide Marxist thinking into that which is contained in Marx and Engel's own writings – classic Marxism – and later theories derived not just from the original writings but also from debate among their followers. There are, of course, many varieties of the latter, but there is no room here to be too precise about the order of succession. Althusser figures so largely in debates about ideology partly because of the distinct historical circumstances that inspired his work: namely the near-revolutionary situation in France in the late 1960s, when it seemed for a time as though the ideal revolutionary alliance of workers and intellectuals was about to ferment. His thinking was founded in a debate about the political role of the universities, and education, and by extension about other dimensions of intellectual life, such as the arts. Pierre Macherey's work (*A Theory of Literary Production*) which you will have studied in relation to *The Outsider* was a development in this debate. Not all Althusser's work has been of use or relevance to literary theorists. Personally he was not even specially interested in the arts, and so it is not practical to introduce you to passages of his work that encapsulate his theories about literature: there is no coherent, workable theory. But some of his ideas have been transferred to the field of aesthetics, and have had considerable influence on literary criticism in the 70s and 80s.

*4.3*  Althusser directed his attention towards social practice – or 'what actually happens'. And for analytical purposes he divided all social practice into three domains: the economic, the political, and the ideological. Of course, *in practice* all three interact, but he separated them out in order to be able to look at them more clearly and see *how* they interact. It is largely because of the diffusion of his influence that we now see as political what we might formerly have seen as ideological – and that we see as ideological so much that used to be thought of as 'natural': for example the constitution of 'literature' and the 'canon' as primarily the work of white, male, middle-class writers, which used to be thought of as natural, is now seen as ideologically constructed, and hence as a political issue. And it is because he separated the ideological from the political and the economic that he exposed to the light certain areas of thought that may not seem to be economically determined or politically circumscribed. And in that exposed area of thought reside the cultural practices we call the arts.

*4.4*  In previous materialist theories, thought was held to proceed from the materialist base, to be organized into coherent sets of beliefs, and then reimposed: an up and back down again movement. But as we have already seen in Section 1, Althusser suggested we should reverse this, and see ideologies *not as what we think, but as what we live*.

*4.5*  But life, in Althusser's view of it as something determined by ideologies of which people are not always conscious, is itself a very different thing from the humanist view of it, which basically sees men and women as in command of their thinking. It is in this idea of *unconscious* determination – where Marx meets Freud – that the theory becomes relevant to the arts.

*4.6* Like Marx (and Marxism), Freud (and Freudianism) are figures and concepts that one needs to know at least a little about before it is possible to achieve even the most rudimentary understanding of twentieth-century thinking.

## Freud

*4.7* Sigmund Freud, who was born in Vienna in 1856 and died in London in 1939, was a psychiatrist and pioneer of psychoanalysis. He first achieved fame (and notoriety) with *Studies in Hysteria* (1895), which proposed the theory that neuroses are rooted in suppressed sexual desires and in the sexual experiences of childhood, either real or imaginary. His view that sexuality originates at birth, not puberty, was particularly controversial.

---

*ACTIVITY*

*The Interpretation of Dreams* (1899) explored and made accessible the symbolic structures of the unconscious mind, and some of the reasons why this work and his techniques of psychoanalysis are applicable to the study of the arts are lucidly set out in the extract from Lionel Trilling's *The Liberal Imagination* (Reader, pp.42–8) which you should read now. The view of Freud it represents is relatively unsophisticated and takes no account, for example, of the ways in which Freud's thinking on gender identity has lead to analysis of gendered repression. But it forms a starting point for ideas that will be pursued in Block 7.

---

*4.8* We are all poets in our dreams. Perhaps not very good or original poets, but if, as Trilling says, 'The unconscious mind in its struggle with the conscious always turns from the general to the concrete and finds the tangible trifle more congenial than the large abstraction', then dreaming is analogous to artistic creation – and 'poetry [is] indigenous to the very condition of the mind'. (You could usefully return to this point when you reach the last section of this block, where Theodor Adorno discusses how the writer with a precise political commitment needs to find quasi-subjective forms of expression, which render the work of art 'autonomous'.) Thus (broadly), as psychoanalysis is to the study of the mind, so explicatory criticism may be to the literary text – though this may be either reductive or revelatory, as Trilling shows by his examples.

*4.9* Although Freud's teaching is not limited to sexuality, it is on the whole fair to assert that he saw the unconscious as the terrain in which those aspects of infantile sexuality that have to be repressed in the social interest continue to operate. Subsequently this terrain has been expanded (by Althusser among others). In a way that is analogous to Freud's theories, we *unconsciously* acquire the ideology that allows us to function socially, by repressing the elements of self-interest within it, and we manifest that ideology *from* our subconscious. You can see here that the acquiring and functioning of 'false consciousness' (see paragraph 1.4) is as 'natural', innate, and inescapable, as the processes (by no means incontrovertible, as you will see in Block 7) that, according to Freud and his successors, govern our sexuality. Again, feminism supplies a useful and vivid example. Patriarchal oppression was not – is not – a systematically conscious form of tyranny. That would be an ideology in the old sense. It was for so long so diffused throughout social practices that it seemed natural and inevitable. On such an issue, even when one's consciousness is 'raised', how one *lives* may still betray that awareness has not reached all the levels of the unconscious. What we can now identify as a prejudice used to seem natural: an ideological conditioning that allows the status quo to be perpetuated without too much rocking of the social boat.

## Althusser

*4.10*  Althusser came to see the function of ideology as the replication of the status quo through social rituals and practices. This, he claimed, is achieved through the connivance of such 'Ideological State Apparatuses' as the educational system, and other social practices in which ideology is produced, transformed, and reconsumed, such as the law, the family and the arts. And literature – its production, consumption and status – can also be seen as just such an area of practice.

*4.11*  But does literature merely reproduce the dominant ideology, transformed, and feed it back again? This is surely a depressingly static view. I prefer to see literature as an arena of contest – a view that is in partial accord with another aspect of Marxist thought, which sees history as the continuing enactment of the class struggle. But it is unrealistic to make exaggerated claims. The mass of literature contests only very timidly; the bourgeois apple-cart may be rocked, but it stays on its wheels. The 'progress' that it records may be only an inch by inch affair, but that, surely, is qualitatively different from a supine reflection of the way things are. Both the plays at the end of this block, for example, were significant political events.

*4.12*  Certainly, Althusser's later position, that there is only one ideology and it functions to preserve the status quo, is a bleak and austere view in which there is little room for challenging, competing or subversive ideas. But is there only one ideology? We are obviously not all motivated by the same self-interests, though mapping how interests and ideologies overlap is a tricky proposition. Here I think Althusser's ideas of a trans-historical 'ideology in general' that is analogous to the subconscious seem to circle round and come back to something oddly like the humanist idea of an eternal principle. Here, he might have said, is an illustration of how we are all trapped within our ideological inheritance. When it came to the arts, he saw Marx as someone who still unwillingly hankered after humanist essentialism. But his own efforts towards a purer materialism eventually led him back to locating the origins of his theory in something external to it. What he does not explain is how 'ideology' as a principle spawned the apparently infinite variety of ideologies that operate and contest within the historical continuum. He seems to see the world as a rather monotonous place in which every activity willingly feeds the dominant ideology. At this point you could take comfort – as I do – from Terry Eagleton's admission that he finds Althusser difficult to follow at times!

*4.13*  Here the views of the earlier Italian Marxist, Antonio Gramsci, are helpful. It was from him that Althusser derived his idea of ideology as that which is lived, but Gramsci did not follow his own premises to such austere conclusions. He maintained that ideology is:

> ... a conception of the world that is implicitly manifest in art, in law, in economic activity and in all manifestations of individual and collective life.
>
> (Gramsci, 1971)

Gramsci argued that the 'spontaneous' ideology of any group or class is incoherent. Effectively, he was attacking the derogatory and hierarchical implications in the idea of 'false consciousness', which had narrowed from Engel's original idea of an inescapable view of our condition, which prevents us seeing the way things really are, to a reductive idea of false consciousness as anything we think or do that contradicts our class interests (see paragraph 1.4). Gramsci – most of whose work was written in a Fascist prison – is among the most humane of Marxist thinkers, and the overriding drive inherent in his theory seems to be a wish to claim for popular thought and action a dignity and even a heroism which are certainly lacking in the severer attitudes of his successors like Althusser.

*4.14* Gramsci recognized that ideology and class interest do not form an exact match, and indeed that the consciousness or ideology of an individual is also fragmented and contradictory. So, in his view, the object of analysing ideological manifestations is to trace the different currents, their confluences and divisions, and the continuing dialectical struggle between them. In his view, there is no single ideology, but an endless variety of complex ideological *formations*. We can see a literary text as just such a formation, where ideologies engage in a dialectical encounter and act out the continuing struggle. All of this block's texts are invigorated by such internal struggles.

## Feminism

*4.15* I have earlier indicated that recent thinking has helped us to see that feminism is an ideological issue, and before moving on to the case-studies where feminist issues are debated, it is important to take this a little further. Personally I think that feminism's re-emergence has been among the most important new thinking to have emerged in the post-war period, and that its influence on literary theory has been of concomitant significance. Now that we can see that the interests of women in any class cannot automatically be identified with those of men, we should perhaps complement the notion of class struggle with 'gender struggle'. Whether or not feminism aspires to become another holistic system like Marxism is itself a moot point, though no feminist today would doubt that there can be any aspect of existence excluded from, or beyond, a feminist reach. But to many feminists the very concepts of a system, of base and superstructure, of dominance and of the material bases of production, are anathema, because they are the thought-products of a male value-system so deeply entrenched that its protagonists cannot locate the ideologically unencumbered ground from which it might be viewed objectively.

*4.16* The Marxist model was based on an industrialized society in which a woman's contribution to the whole cultural and commercial economy was exclusively related – and subordinate – to male effort. Most women of course refuse to claim that the repository of non-material values is located in the feminine – partly because that is a bait too often laid for them. But many also resist a model based (perhaps unconsciously, since Marx could hardly help being a man of his own times) on *men's* work – which women may do as well – rather than *women's* work, which men on the whole do not share.

*4.17* Women are, of course, at least as subject to economic forces as men. But many feminists have reacted against the hyper-rationalism that characterizes classic Marxism, arguing that rationality is a value produced and endorsed by a largely male-dominated educational system, to which women have had comparatively little access. On the other hand, some feminists can accommodate the Althusserian concept of ideology more readily: we have already seen that the very oppression of which women complain is a naturalized ideology. We have also seen that ideology in this sense operates from the unconscious, rather than from the rational domain. Feminists hardly need to reclaim the irrational; it is traditionally – and often pejoratively – thought of as a woman's sphere. But they have learnt to occupy that territory more unapologetically. If ideology is what we live, then – if we also accept Freud – there is inevitably an irrational domain to it. Trilling says 'Freud

showed ... how the mind, in one of its parts, could work without logic'
(Reader, p.47).

*4.18* By now you may be reeling. I have tried to take you with me through a
synthesis that brings together aspects of Marxism, Freudianism, and feminism
– and you may have embarked on the course because you simply enjoyed
reading literature! Indeed, we hope you did. But analysing the sources of
pleasure is more complicated. We began this block with an optimistic,
rationalist programme, and both the case-studies and this theoretical excursion
have taken us into the unconscious and the irrational. Perhaps in studying the
arts we travel hopefully, but do not really hope to arrive. For if we ever did
arrive at a theory that managed to explain the effects of art, then perhaps the
pleasures of exploration would be at an end.

# 5   Spark: 'The Prime of Miss Jean Brodie'

## ACTIVITY

I imagine that you've come across Miss Jean Brodie before now and that you
will read or re-read the novel with preconceptions. We cannot finally escape
from preconceptions: they are still part of every re-reading, no matter how
hard we try to bury them. But please, as you re-read the novel now, try to
put yourself in the position of an intelligent reader from Mars or from a
couple of centuries hence, when the peculiarities of British middle-class mores
in the twentieth century will be hard to understand.

(a)   Who are the main characters in the novel and which of their
characteristics would be obvious to such a distant reader?

(b)   In terms of personal conduct, ethics, morality – what is the theme of the
novel?

(c)   What systems of political and religious belief are foregrounded?

(d)   In what respect is the narrative technique unusual?

Please treat this seriously as an exercise. If your answers differ from my own,
don't conclude that they're wrong. Try to justify them, and see if that works –
you may have noticed points that have escaped me.

## DISCUSSION

(a)   The chief characters are: Miss Jean Brodie, an Edinburgh woman born in
1890 with an unusual approach to school-teaching, and Sandy Stranger,
the daughter of English incomers to the city, who is her pupil, born
about 1920. Jean Brodie has dark, 'Roman' good looks and is strongly
attracted to Italy. We are given to understand that 'in her prime' her
attitudes and behaviour are changing. Thus, though she will not 'commit
adultery' with a married man, she is prepared to sleep with a bachelor.
Sandy is characterized by her small piggy eyes and well developed
fantasy life. She feels like an outsider in Edinburgh (a point which her
surname reinforces). She is fascinated by sex, enters a relationship with
the married man whom Miss Brodie loves, but eventually becomes a nun.
Highly intelligent, she gets Miss Brodie dismissed from her teaching job
for preaching right-wing politics.

If you concluded that several of the 'Brodie set' and certain of Miss Brodie's colleagues are important characters, I can see why. My summary above leaves out entirely a feature that would surely strike an intelligent Martian – the novel's concern with school life, with relationships not only between pupils and teachers, but also within both groups.

(b) Again, I can see why you might have concluded that 'sex' or 'adultery' is the novel's main ethical concern. But I would propose the word 'betrayal'. We learn early in the book that Miss Brodie will be 'betrayed'.

(c) I wouldn't expect disagreement over the 'political' and 'religious' content of the book. Clearly, 'Fascism' is one of its concerns. The dominant spirit of Edinburgh is conceived to be informed by Calvinistic Presbyterianism, and Sandy is converted to Catholicism.

(d) The most striking feature of the narrative is surely its toing and froing over a period of thirty years. It starts in 1936, soon jumps back to 1930, then on page 15 we learn of Mary Macgregor's death in 1943. Returning to 1939, we move forward to 1931, jump to 1959, back to 1931… Notice that this affects the element of 'suspense', which in this book, as in most fiction, is important. We know very early in the book that Miss Brodie will be 'betrayed'. By page 60 we know that Sandy is the 'traitor'. Yet an element of suspense remains. We do not know what prompted the betrayal till very near the end of the book, and the details of Jean Brodie's relations with Lloyd and Lowther are unfolded to us suspensefully – we don't know what will happen next or in the long run.

---

5.1   So we have before us a novel dominated by female characters, in which 'moral' themes are strongly present, one that implicitly contrasts two versions of Christian belief and involves politics prominently. Its narrative technique is complex and unusual. It is so short (128 pages in paperback) that it might be described as a 'novella'. This book treats a wide range of material over a time span of nearly 30 years in a highly compressed way. It could be tempting to see it as ordered by oppositions:

| | |
|---|---|
| progressive (Brodie) | conventional (Mackay) |
| unselfcritical (Brodie) | self-critical (Sandy) |
| pro-Fascist (Brodie) | anti-Fascist (Sandy) |
| Calvinistic (Brodie) | Catholic (Sandy) |

5.2   But to sort things out this way (a technique that works for much fiction, even for such a huge novel as *War and Peace*) shows how complex Spark's patterning is. Our Martian reader is puzzled to note that the conventions that Jean Brodie opposes are related to Calvinism and that Sandy rejects Miss Brodie's authority (and her Fascist sympathies) in favour of strict religious discipline. This novel does not easily yield a 'message'.

5.3   I live in Edinburgh. From the window of the study where I'm writing, I look towards the dowdily imposing buildings of James Gillespie's School, currently a comprehensive school controlled by Lothian Regional Council, but once a fee-paying establishment for girls attended by Muriel Spark, and without doubt the 'original' of 'Marcia Blaine's' in her novel. If I go to my nearest Safeway Supermarket, I pass Church Hill where Miss Jean Brodie lives. Proceeding in the opposite direction, I can and do descend into the Grassmarket like the Brodie girls on their educational walk before climbing up, as they do, to St Giles'. On the way, I will pass Deacon Brodie's Tavern, named after Miss Brodie's illustrious forebear.

5.4   Deacon Brodie helped to inspire *Dr Jekyll and Mr Hyde*, by the Edinburgh-born Robert Louis Stevenson, a writer evoked directly and quoted without attribution in Spark's novel. In late eighteenth-century Edinburgh, William Brodie was a prosperous cabinet maker and property owner, a Deacon of his Guild and a Town Councillor. He was also a gambler who had separate families by two mistresses. In 1788, it came out that for some time, with a mask over his face, he had been leading a gang of robbers which had attacked local shops. The gang tried and failed to rob the General Excise Office. A member betrayed Brodie, who was convicted and hanged before thousands of people in the High Street, west of St. Giles. In his respectable days he himself had redesigned and improved the halter which he helped the executioner slip over his own head.

5.5   If the Deacon seems like an invention of some extravagant fictive imagination, his putative descendant, Jean Brodie, has infiltrated 'real life'. Miss Brodie's initial appearance in prose (in the *New Yorker* magazine, 1961) was followed by her exploitation on stage and screen. She was played by those wonderful (English) actresses Vanessa Redgrave and (in a feature film) Maggie Smith. Having been dark haired and Italianate in Spark's novel, she became blonde and rather Nordic. Her subsequent appearance as heroine of a TV series (Geraldine McEwan) extended our biographical knowledge of her beyond Spark's original text. Like Falstaff and Pickwick, Sherlock Holmes and Jeeves, she has gone on and on by popular demand. Like them, she signifies a peculiar cluster of qualities and accidents.

5.6   What are these? Imperiousness, dogmatism, eccentricity, the capacity to cast a spell over schoolgirls and male admirers. In Scotland, she is identified with 'Morningside', a term which, like 'Hampstead', is not limited in application to residents of the suburb in question. 'Morningside Ladies' are as common in Corstorphine or Blackhall. 'Morningside' is where 'sex' is what the coalman brings his wares in, an arena of Anglicized gentility. With all this, Miss Brodie elicits affection, as the drunken, thieving, cowardly Falstaff does. Her absurdity, and her ultimate frailty, are endearing.

## Ideology and history

5.7   In 1979 Spark said:

> I am certainly a writer of Scottish formation and of course think of myself as one ... Edinburgh, where I was born and my father was born has definitely had an effect on my mind, my prose style and my ways of thought.
>
> (quoted in Bold, 1984, p.26)

In 1988, she told the Scottish branch of the writers' association PEN, 'Edinburgh was my whole world for the first 19 years of my life and it has been my constant point of departure and return for the rest of it' (reported in *The Scotsman*, 10 September 1988). The complexity of her attitude towards Edinburgh emerges from an essay she published in 1970 (Millar, 1970, pp.151–3): 'Edinburgh is the place that I, a constitutional exile, am essentially exiled from...'

5.8   She was born Muriel Sarah Camberg in 1918. Her father was a Jewish engineer, her mother the daughter of a Hertfordshire shopkeeper. As with Sandy in her novel (though rather less so), aspects of her family background made her a 'stranger'. Yet she claims to have been happy at James Gillespie's Girls School, which, 'set in solid state among the green meadows, showed an energetic faith in my literary life. I was the school's poet and dreamer, with appropriate perquisites and concessions'.

5.9   She describes herself as a 'puritanically nurtured soul' – in tune, that is, with Edinburgh's Presbyterian ethos, approving of 'puritan virtues' such as industriousness, horror of debt, 'polite reticence about sex', which are regarded as eccentric in the south of England.

*5.10* Most interestingly of all she discusses the effect on her of Edinburgh usage of the word 'nevertheless':

> All grades of society constructed sentences bridged by 'nevertheless'... I believe myself to be fairly indoctrinated with the habit of thought which calls for this word. In fact I approve of the ceremonious accumulation of weather forecasts and barometer readings that pronounces for a fine day, before letting rip on the statement, 'Nevertheless, it's raining'. I find that much of my literary composition is based on the nevertheless idea. I act upon it. It was on the nevertheless principle that I turned Catholic.
>
> (quoted in Millar, 1970, pp.151–3)

She associates the 'nevertheless principle' with the most obviously dramatic feature of Edinburgh, the Castle Hill dominating its centre. 'To have a great primitive black crag rising up in the middle of populated streets of commerce, stately squares and winding closes, is like the statement of an unmitigated fact preceded by "nevertheless".' The Castle seems to represent, for her, human sinfulness standing in apposition to all the business and beauty of the city.

*5.11* But if the image means something like this to her, why become a Catholic rather than embracing the Calvinist doctrines which stress the ubiquity of sin, the likelihood of damnation? How does Edinburgh inspire someone to turn to a creed alien to the city's traditions? Spark's dealings with religion in *Miss Jean Brodie* may provide cryptic hints of explanation. Miss Brodie herself represents a cast of mind derived from Calvinism, which, partly because she has no theology, has tragi-comic consequences. A logical person such as Spark was, sincerely attracted by Christianity, though Jewish, would not find in the Edinburgh 'Calvinism' of her youth a satisfactory answer. Presbyterianism was *socially* dominant, *ethically* on top. But, the Church of Scotland had in effect abandoned Calvinist orthodoxy, had replaced theology with homilies, eschatological vision with petty prudery.

*5.12* Muriel Camberg left Edinburgh for Rhodesia (now Zimbabwe) where she married S.O. Spark. In 1944, having divorced her husband, she went to work at Woburn Abbey in the British 'Black Propaganda' department which invented lies to deceive the German enemy. Then she moved around in the literary circles of post-war London, briefly acting as secretary of the Poetry Society (she was dismissed for being too adventurous). She had written poetry since the age of nine, her first book (1952) was a 'slim volume' of poetry, but after a short story by her won first prize, out of 6,700 entries, in a Christmas story competition run by *The Observer* newspaper, she was commissioned to write a novel. In 1954, the year she was received into the Roman Catholic Church, she began work on *The Comforter*. This and four other novels earned her a very high reputation, before the *New Yorker* published, in one of its issues, the whole of *Miss Jean Brodie*. In 1962 she left Britain, first for New York, then for Italy, where she has lived since 1966. More than a dozen novels have followed *MJB*.

*5.13* Until *Symposium* (1990), it was her only novel set in Scotland, and *MJB*'s vast success in England and North America suggests that it deals with characters and themes of interest outside Scotland. '*Nevertheless*', its Edinburgh setting, and the historical period it presents, are surely of great importance. Spark is on record as being greatly concerned with accuracy of detail. As with any novelist dealing with 'history', though, what she leaves out may be as significant as what she includes.

*5.14* *Miss Jean Brodie* (henceforward *MJB*) is centred on the 1930s. That decade is remembered as a period of unemployment and poverty for many. Historians have argued over what stress should be placed – were the thirties, on the whole, bad times or good times? As you know from looking at Auden, the literature produced by younger writers during the period insists on its being a time of crisis. 'Taking sides on the Spanish Civil War', in particular, seemed imperative – as in *MJB*.

5.15   In Scotland, the great heavy industries – shipbuilding, engineering, steel, coal – were in dire trouble. The Labour Party had gained ground. Communists were more influential than in England. The Scottish National Party, founded in 1928, won few votes in elections, but attracted significant intellectuals.

5.16   But Edinburgh was relatively little affected by all these developments. The city's politics were predominantly conservative. Sectarian Protestant feeling against Catholics of Irish origin was a major issue in local elections. There was a violent riot in the douce suburb of Morningside in 1936 when the Catholic hierarchy arranged a rally in Canaan Lane Park, and 35,000 or 40,000 Protestants encircled it. In the November elections of that year, 'Protestant Action' reached a zenith, with nine seats on the City Council, and 32 per cent of the vote – Labour took under 30 per cent and the 'Moderates', generally conservative, 38.2 per cent. PA's leader, Cormack, had a special cadre called Kormack's Kaledonian Klan, borrowing symbols as well as initials from the white racist Ku Klux Klan of the southern states of the US (Bruce, 1985, pp.88–91, 97).

5.17   As a Jewish girl on her way to becoming a Catholic, Spark can hardly have been unaware of the strength of quasi-Fascist Protestant feeling in her native city. Her omission of any mention of it suggests that she felt compelled to simplify the pattern of 30s history.

5.18   Brodie is fascistic, not sectarian. However, it is not fortuitous that she is betrayed as a pro-Fascist by a pupil who chooses Catholicism. British Catholics might well 'take sides' against the Spanish Republic, whose supporters were largely anti-clerical and were accused of atrocities against the Church. Sandy's political choice, against Fascism, is not logically connected with her religious choice. Nevertheless, by choosing Rome, Sandy is implicitly rejecting genteel and not-so-genteel Presbyterian Edinburgh, which had its own fascistic tinge.

5.19   But as you know, Auden, himself a schoolteacher, was, by his own admission, close to Fascism in the early thirties. Such far-from-negligible figures as Churchill, G.B. Shaw and H.G. Wells expressed at one time or another admiration for Mussolini, or Stalin, and the role of the Great Leader. The cult of the Great Man was not the property of the traditional right. Brodie brings before us the *ambiguity* of thirties' commitment. Whether one favoured the Stalinist or Nazi variety of 'planning' as a way of getting rid of unemployment was not a matter of obvious choice.

5.20   It should be clear by now that the involvement of 'ideology' in *MJB* is unusually complex. We might usefully separate four different 'levels'.

(a)   The author's own 'ideas' are of valid interest. She is well known to be a Catholic convert. Yet the handling of Catholicism in the book hardly suggests a proselytising aim: Sandy's conversion does not seem to make her happy. Likewise, Muriel Spark is on record as stating that her own school days were, for her, good days, and that Edinburgh meant and means a lot to her. Nevertheless, the presentation of school and city in her novel is sharply critical.

(b)   Jean Brodie attaches herself to Fascist 'ideology', using the word in its conventional sense: 'a bad, wrong-headed set of theories.'

(c)   If we begin to explore 'ideology' in the novel in the broader 'Althusserian' sense of the word, we find that it presents a 'bourgeois' environment to us, characterized by the cult of respectability, by sexual prudery, and by a conception of female education that takes for granted that girls will perform certain roles and not others when they grow up. Jean Brodie and Sandy both challenge this prevailing ideology, though Jean Brodie is partly implicated in it.

(d)  Finally, Jean Brodie and Sandy are both *story-tellers*. The making of fictional alternatives to 'reality' is itself a theme of this fiction. The place of fiction *inside* and *outside* 'ideology' is an issue raised by the telling of Spark's story.

*5.21*  Attempting to clarify 'ideology' in *MJB*, I have been helped by two theorists, both Marxist.

*5.22*  Firstly Antonio Gramsci, who was discussed in Section 4. This powerful thinker has been seminal in much recent writing about cultural questions. (As you may remember, for the last ten years of his life – 1926 to 1936 – he was imprisoned by Mussolini, the *Duce* adored by Jean Brodie.) Gramsci distinguished between 'historically organic ideologies' – those necessary to a given structure – and 'ideologies that are arbitrary, rationalistic, or "willed"':

> To the extent that ideologies are historically necessary they have a validity that is 'psychological'; they 'organize' human masses, and create the terrain on which men move, acquire consciousness of their position, struggle, and so on. To the extent that they are arbitrary they only create individual 'movements', polemics and so on (though even these are not completely useless, since they function like an error which, by contrasting with truth, demonstrates it.
>
> (Gramsci, 1971 p.377)

*5.23*  Gramsci's argument helps me to perceive that Jean Brodie's 'arbitrary' and 'willed' ideology, Fascism, stands in tragi-comic relationship to the 'organic' ideology of the *Edimbourgeoisie*.

*5.24*  A second useful quotation comes from Pierre Macherey, whose work you considered in relation to *The Outsider*. His view of 'ideology', as mere false consciousness, is very different from Gramsci's, but helps me put my finger on the ultra-*literary* quality of Spark's text:

> ...the autonomy of the writer's discourse is established from its relationship with the other uses of language: everyday speech, scientific propositions. By its energy and thinness literary discourse mimics theoretical discourse ... But in that evocative power, by which it denotes a specific reality, it also imitates the everyday language which is the language of ideology. We could offer a provisional definition of literature as being characterized by this power of parody...
>
> (Macherey, 1978, p.59)

In Macherey's school of thought, 'science' (i.e. Marxism) opposes 'ideology' (false consciousness) and 'literature' stands in between, performing the useful role of exposing ideology, though not by 'scientific' procedures. It produces 'the analogy of a knowledge' and 'a caricature of customary ideology'. One does not need to share Macherey's faith in Marxist 'science' (in contrast with Gramsci's practice-rooted thought, it seems to me superstitious!) to see value in his definition of the 'space' in which 'literature works', and within this space, *MJB* 'works' stupendously hard. The novel not only 'parodies' everyday life and 'customary ideology', it also 'parodies' more than one 'literary' or 'sub-literary' or 'pseudo-literary' discourse, in the stories 'made up' by Jean Brodie and Sandy. Spark is quizzical about 'realism' in fiction, to the point of seeming almost inimical to it. 'Realistic fiction' at its most trivial merely imitates the 'customary', seeks to 'reflect' social life permeated with 'ideology'. Spark is concerned not with 'imitation' but, like Sandy, with 'transfiguration' of the 'commonplace'.

5.25   What makes Spark's fictional construction 'Miss Brodie' vivid, memorable, lovable up to a point, is her semi-conscious attempt, analogous to the 'literary' writer's project, to 'transfigure the commonplace'. Comedy and pathos both arise from the incapacity of her language (unlike Spark's) to escape from 'customary ideology'.

## Class in *Miss Jean Brodie*

5.26   In the 'classic' Marxist view 'classes' are defined by their relationship to the means of production. Under modern capitalism the bourgeoisie own these, wage workers own nothing but their labour power. It is possible to disagree with all or part of Marx's theory, while still regarding 'class' as a key factor in social, political and cultural life. Thus Arthur Marwick contends, in his survey *Class: Image and Reality*, that:

> Industrial societies were, and are, grossly unequal in the distribution of power, wealth, income and life chances, and contain marked distinctions in behaviour and lifestyles. The different images of class held by different individuals and different groups roughly coincide with the broad bands of inequality and distinctions which can be objectively established.
>
> (Marwick, 1980, p.359)

What Marwick calls 'the language of class' is a potent presence in ideology.

## *ACTIVITY*

Could you please sort the characters in *MJB* into 'upper', 'middle' and 'lower' social strata.

## *DISCUSSION*

Only two characters might qualify as 'upper class'. Gordon Lowther is a 'man of substance' who lives in a mansion (pp.88–9); Joyce Emily Hammond lives 'in a huge house with a stable'. Significantly, the girls at Marcia Blaine's disapprove of her partly because of her 'shiny car and chauffeur' (pp.116–17). Though it is clear that she is 'very rich' (p.8) we do not know for certain that she is 'well born' or 'well bred'. Lowther's wealth, on the other hand, is clearly inherited. His 'upper-class' status may explain his self-consciously 'un-Edinburgh conduct' in twitching Jenny's ringlets (p.23). However, as music teacher and as choirmaster and elder of the Church of Scotland, he is integrated into the 'Edinburgh' milieu typified by Marcia Blaine's.

This milieu is overwhelmingly 'middle class'. Though parents pay to send their children to the school, its education is acquired at 'endowed rates' – families of modest means can afford it. The school isn't snobbish in a gross way. It accommodates girls of a wide range of backgrounds, including Rose whose father runs an 'extensive shoe-making business' but 'proudly' professes himself 'a cobbler' (p.119), and Jenny whose father has a grocer's shop. Sandy's English mother is marked as an outsider by her wearing a 'flashy winter coat trimmed with fluffy fox fur ... while the other mothers wore tweed or, at the most, musquash that would do them all their days' (p.18).

Critics sometimes write as if Marcia Blaine's is a repressive institution. That is Jean Brodie's view of it. But it seems, for its time, quite a progressive establishment. The headmistress, however unpleasant in other respects, at least encourages the 'Modern' subjects so despised by Miss Brodie. We learn (p.83) that the history teacher is 'a vegetarian communist', and Miss Brodie herself sneers that the Senior teachers 'all belong to the Fabian Society and are pacifists' (p.107). Such details modify – one might say 'mitigate' – the implications of the phrase 'petty-bourgeois' which so readily attaches itself to this little world in which the daughters of families of middling means are being trained for life and *perhaps* for work.

The third social stratum identifiable in the novel consists of *the unemployed*. In Sandy's delicious interview with the Lady of Shalott (p.21) the latter refers to 'some heedless member of the Unemployed', which suggests that Sandy's middle-class parents blame, as many such did in the thirties, the fecklessness of the poor as the cause of their joblessness. 'The Unemployed' is conceived as a 'class' with 'members'. Monica Douglas's background is such that she refers to the 'Unemployed' as 'the Idle'. Jean Brodie calls on her set to pray for them and asserts 'they are our brothers' but even so she repeats the familiar slur that: 'Sometimes they go and spend their dole on drink before they go home, and their children starve' (p.39).

## ACTIVITY

The 'Unemployed' cluster in the 'reeking network of slums' to which Jean Brodie leads her pupils, conceived by them as 'a misty region of crime and desperation'. Please re-read the short passage (pp.32–3) which describes the Grassmarket and then turn to the paragraph beginning 'Miss Brodie telephoned...' at the foot of page 122.

## DISCUSSION

These passages seem to me to be important in directing our sympathies between Sandy and Jean Brodie. Miss Brodie's only interest is in the 'history' of the Old Town. She approves of the abolition (which she attributes to Mussolini) of unemployment. But she has no interest in the lives and characters of the poor. Jean Brodie's grandiose faith that Hitler will 'save the world' is contested by Sandy's hope – more 'realistic' in every way – that 'the poor people' will be 'relieved'. It is very difficult in this novel, as in Spark's fiction generally, to decide where the novelist wants our sympathies to go. But here, surely, we must side with Sandy against her teacher who, even in 1946, can only concede that 'Hitler *was* rather naughty'.

5.27   So 'class' is rather more central to the novel than a quick, casual reading might suggest. However, it is pushed, on the whole, out of sight not only by the gender of most of the main characters, but by the ideological construction, 'Edinburgh'.

5.28   Mr Lowther indulges in 'un-Edinburgh' conduct. The Lloyds are clearly 'un-Edinburgh' – he is not only, by reports, 'half Welsh, half English' (p.48), but Catholic to boot. His wife, Deirdre, as Jean Brodie suggests in her one word comment on her name – 'Celtic' – is tainted with the dreadful stigma of Irishness. She anticipates fashion by wearing a 'peasant skirt' and her request 'pass me a fag' (p.103) amplifies her 'Bohemian' aura.

5.29   In the other camp we have the Junior teachers who say 'good morning' to Miss Brodie, after her own looseness of morals is suspected, in a 'more than Edinburgh' manner (p.54). 'Edinburgh' as an adjective signifies 'middle-class Protestant'. And Miss Brodie, willy nilly, is 'Edinburgh'. In the midst of her imitation of a Roman gladiator she breaks off to complain that someone has opened the window too wide: 'Six inches is perfectly adequate. More is vulgar' (p.46). She will not let Eunice do cartwheels in her house on Sundays because 'in many ways' she is an 'Edinburgh spinster of the deepest dye' (p.26). Italophile though she is, love Teddy Lloyd as she may, she is anti-Catholic. She is not simply 'bourgeois' or 'petty bourgeois' she is *Edimbourgeois* and 'Edinburgh'.

## ACTIVITY

Please re-read the very important paragraph beginning 'Fully to savour her position...' on page 108, where the term 'class' occurs, its only significant appearance in the novel. Note down any points that occur to you.

## DISCUSSION

Sandy's own 'class' position is rather cryptically defined. We may infer that the class 'just above' her own would include the well-to-do 'New Town' lawyers, bankers, financiers and (perhaps) professors who gave the city its permanently-resident 'upper' crust. Being in many cases part-Anglicized, the ethos of these people is less 'peculiar' to Edinburgh than that of the class 'just below' ('grocers', 'cobblers'). Sandy has failed to appreciate this peculiarity. Now she feels deprived of 'some quality of life peculiar to Edinburgh'. And this is associated, for her, with 'the religion of Calvin'.

### *Miss Jean Brodie* and predestination

*5.30  MJB* is an extremely funny novel in places. *Nevertheless*, it takes up a rather grim religious position. I agree with David Lodge that it carries 'a severe and uncompromising dogmatic message: that all groups, communions and institutions are false and more or less corrupting except the one that is founded on the truths of Christian orthodoxy – and even that one is not particularly attractive or virtuous' (Lodge, p.135). 'Predestination' and 'grace', crucial concepts in Christian theology, jut from Spark's text as the Castle Hill juts into the Edinburgh skyline: *nevertheless*. 'If we are not ashamed of the Gospel', according to John Calvin, the sixteenth-century French theologian whose views, by 1643, had become Church of Scotland orthodoxy, 'we must confess what is there plainly declared. God, by His eternal goodwill, which has no cause outside itself, destined those whom He pleased to salvation, rejecting the rest: those whom he dignified by gratuitous adoption He illumined by His Spirit, so that they receive the life offered in Christ, while others voluntarily disbelieve, so that they remain in darkness destitute of the light of faith' (Calvin, 1961, p.58). This creed had been challenged by two of the most powerful Scottish writers – by Burns in 'Holy Willie's Prayer' and James Hogg in a very remarkable novel, *The Confessions of a Justified Sinner.* The thrust of both men can be summarized thus: those who believe themselves to be saved by the 'eternal goodwill' of God are likely to fall into 'antinomianism' – the heresy of believing oneself to be exempt from moral laws applicable to humankind in general. 'Holy' Willie can fornicate, Hogg's *Justified Sinner* can murder, secure in the knowledge that they are 'elect'.

*5.31*  Antinomianism results in 'double lives'. 'Doubleness' and 'doubling' are important factors in nineteenth-century fiction: Dostoevsky makes particularly elaborate and frequent use of them. But no 'doubles' are more famous than Robert Louis Stevenson's Dr Jekyll and Mr Hyde. Spark is writing within a strong Scottish tradition when she has Miss Brodie lead a 'double life', like her famous Brodie forebear.

*5.32* One aspect of 'doubleness' in Miss Brodie is the apparent dichotomy between the 'unfinished quality' that Sandy detects in her (p.71) and her 'absolute' self-confidence, her fixity. Unlike her fellow teachers she is 'outwardly' still in 'a state of fluctuating development' whereas they have 'only too understandably not trusted themselves to change their minds, particularly on ethical questions, after the age of twenty' (p.43). She does not act like a creature whose behaviour is predetermined: 'the principles governing the end of her prime would have astonished herself at the beginning of it' (p.44). It is touching that she should ask her own pupils to teach her Greek as they learn it themselves, yet characteristic that she should be heard declaring, soon after we learn of this, that 'Everyone knows what a straight line and a circle are', and that she should give her girls to understand that the solution to arithmetic problems 'would be quite useless to Sybil Thorndike, Anna Pavlova and the late Helen of Troy' (p.82). Many of her characteristic sayings imply that she is utterly unshakeable in her belief that all her opinions are right.

*5.33* As Faith Pullin has pointed out, 'her decisions are always couched in religious terms: she "renounces" Mr Lloyd because he is married, she "dedicates" herself to Mr Lowther and to her girls' (Bold, 1984, p.89). The 'rigid Edinburgh-born side of herself' rejects Catholicism, but she is tolerant towards all Protestant sects, going to a church of a different denomination each Sunday. However, her mental set, as Sandy comes to perceive, is Calvinist and antinomian. 'She was not in any doubt, she let everyone know she was in no doubt, that God was on her side whatever her course' (p.85). She believes that Rose will be a great lover and as such entitled to act 'above the moral laws'. Sandy betrays Jean Brodie primarily because of this ultra-antinomianism: 'She thinks she is Providence, thought Sandy, she thinks she is the God of Calvin, she sees the beginning and the end.'

*5.34* In 1927, when the Nazi Party was still far from power, Hitler's lieutenant, Rudolf Hess, wrote: 'the Führer must be absolute in his propaganda speeches. He must not weigh up the pros and cons like an academic, he must never leave his listeners the freedom to think something else is right...' Ian Kershaw comments that the 'fawning devotion' displayed by Hess himself represents 'a search for a secular instead of a religious faith'. As the Nazis gained momentum in the early thirties, Hitler was being portrayed as 'the leader of the coming Germany'. Over-enthusiastic followers freely compared him to Jesus Christ. A Nazi journal described his participation at a conference of Party functionaries as a 'sacred experience' (Kershaw, 1987, pp.27, 38–9).

*5.35* This aspect of Nazism is highly relevant to Sandy's earlier doubts about Miss Brodie. We've already noted the crucial importance of Sandy's confrontation with the Old Town poor. An earlier spectacle on the girls' walk, that of a group of Girl Guides with a 'regimented vigorous look', elicits Miss Brodie's most wonderful saying: 'For those who like that sort of thing, that is the sort of thing they like.' But Sandy thinks of Miss Brodie's admiration for Mussolini's *fascisti* and it occurs to her that 'the Brodie set' is 'Miss Brodie's fascisti ... all knit together for her need' (p.31). Later in the same walk, the 'double' Miss Brodie is heard explaining that her principles of education involve leading out only, as opposed to Miss Mackay who believes in 'putting in' – 'intrusion'. She reverts to this subject after her next visit to Italy: '...Mussolini has performed feats of magnitude and unemployment is even further abolished under him than it was last year ... Education means a leading out from *e*, out, and *duco*, I lead.' But Mussolini, of course, was *Il Duce*.

*5.36* 'In one aspect of propaganda', writes Anthony Rhodes, '...the Fascists always remained the equal of, if not superior to, the Nazis – the education of the young.' The curriculum was revised so that all children learnt their duties as Fascist citizens: 'Teachers were required to take an oath of loyalty to the regime, or risk dismissal' (Rhodes, 1987, pp.71–2). The 'doubleness' of Miss Brodie is nowhere more salient than in the passages cited above. On the one hand she professes an ultra-liberal view of education, as a free and non-coercive process. On the other, she is a 'leader' and her play with the Latin *duco* associates her with Fascist dictatorship. Not content with breaking the conventional moral code of 'Edinburgh' in her relationship with Lowther, she breaks her *own* self-defined law, intruding Fascism into Joyce Emily's head. This is the summit of antinomianism.

5.37   When, on that walk (p.30), Sandy looks back at her companions and understands them 'as a body with Miss Brodie for the head', all 'in unified compliance to the destiny of Miss Brodie, as if God had willed them to both for that purpose', there is, as David Lodge has pointed out, a concealed religious metaphor: '…an allusion to the doctrine of the Church as the Mystical Body of Christ … of which Christ himself is the head…' The Church implied here is, however, a Calvinistic one, built on the ideas of election and predestination (Lodge, op. cit., p.136; the relevant biblical passages are found in I Corinthians 11 and 12).

5.38   Miss Brodie is set up as a false prophet, a pseudo-Christ, an anti-Christ. Her error of political judgement (pro-Fascism) might nowadays seem a small enough sin in the sight of God (after all, many, many Europeans made the same mistake). But the God-mimicking that leads to Joyce Emily's death is eternally heretical and evil.

5.39   As Sandy sees it, Brodie thus betrays her own set. Sandy tells Miss Brodie at their last meeting: 'If you did not betray us it is impossible that you could have been betrayed by us. The word betrayed does not apply…' Later she tells Monica, 'It's only possible to betray where loyalty is due' (pp.126–7). But do we accept that Sandy's 'putting a stop' to Brodie is thus justified?

5.40   Orthodox Catholic theologians would argue that God has *foreknowledge* of everything, but that He invites His creations, human beings, to share the freedom that He enjoys. So the future, though known to Him, is not *preordained*.

5.41   As Valerie Shaw points out, Cardinal Newman, a nineteenth-century Catholic convert whose writings deeply influenced Spark, argues that Calvinism's 'sharp separation between the elect and the world contains much that is cognate or parallel to the catholic doctrine', but for Roman Catholics the dogma is 'shaded and softened' by the notion of 'different degrees' of justification. 'There is no certain knowledge given to anyone that he is simply in a state of grace' (Cairns Craig, 1988, p.281). It is characteristic of Spark to leave her readers with radical doubts about which (if any) of her fictional characters is in a state of grace, even in the non-theological sense of simply earning the novelist's and reader's approval and good will.

5.42   Sandy, as a nun, is likely to be in a 'state of grace' as Catholics see it. But our confidence in her spiritual authority is undermined because she seems uneasy, unhappy in the convent.

5.43   From page 8 when *Sandy* looks back to see Joyce Emily walk and skip away, her consciousness is 'privileged' within the novel. We are therefore inclined to believe that her judgements have the author's own weight behind them and that what she perceives, and her interpretation of her perceptions, are 'true'. Yet a trail of hints sabotages her authority. Her small pig-like eyes do not metaphorically suggest broad or generous vision. On page 34 when Sandy appears as a nun, her memory is shown to be at fault – she recalls being taken for a walk 'through the Canongate', but Miss Brodie's route leads through the Grassmarket up to St Giles Kirk and along Chambers Street and does not include the Canongate. Much more decisive is her interrogation of Monica over Lloyd's embrace of Brodie. 'Which arm?' Sandy snapped.

'The right of course, he hasn't got a left' (p.51). Sandy is shown here as a clever girl, prone, when agitated, to lose touch with reality. The 'creeping vision of disorder' from which she is recovering in the nunnery hints at a disorder in her own vision (p.86). Yet it is her vision that is our authority for the important perception that all Lloyd's portraits look like Miss Brodie. Spark's narrator is, in this phase, ironical about Sandy listening to the Lloyds' conversation and 'calculating their souls by signs and symbols, as was the habit in those days of young persons who had read books of psychology'. Are not psychologists like Freud and Jung as much false prophets as Miss Brodie when set against the true dogma of Catholicism?

5.44   A Jesuit, non-Catholics may feel, would have no trouble accommodating Freud if it seemed worth while. It is possible to relate both Jean Brodie and Sandy to real or supposed Jesuit characteristics. It is Miss Brodie who echoes the Jesuit educational credo when she proclaims 'give me a girl at an impressionable age, and she is mine for life' (p.9). But it is Sandy who displays 'Jesuitical' casuistry when she betrays her teacher. 'You won't be able to pin her down on sex. Have you thought of politics?' (p.124).

5.45   Should we forgive Sandy? Is it not harder to forgive a self-critical person who cold-bloodedly 'puts a stop' to the career of a once-loved teacher than to condone the behaviour of self-deceiving, unselfcritical Miss Brodie? Paradoxically it is easier to forgive Sandy if one sees *her* behaviour as largely determined by Brodie, her teaching, and Sandy's reaction against it: sleeping with Lloyd in Rose's place, and so absorbing his Catholicism.

5.46   The most 'innocent' person in the novel is surely Mary Macgregor, who gets blamed for everything. Ironically, Mary looks back just before her death on 'the first years with Miss Brodie' as 'the happiest time of her life' (p.15). Her innocence is, of course, allied to extreme stupidity. But Sandy's self-critical cleverness guarantees her loss of innocence.

## ACTIVITY

David Lodge draws attention to certain details in Spark's account of the last meeting of Miss Brodie and Sandy (Lodge, 1971, pp.143–4). Please now re-read the account of this meeting (pp.55–6, 60). What do you make of Spark's evocation of the hills seen from the hotel?

## DISCUSSION

They are associated, as Lodge points out, with the 'everlasting hills' referred to in Genesis 49:26 (Authorized Version). Lodge suggests that their association with 'the first and unbetrayable' Miss Brodie expresses 'Sandy's nostalgia for a lost primal innocence, her regret that, the world being what it is, Miss Brodie's good qualities are so mixed with bad that she had to be betrayed'.

While the religious issues in *MJB* are paramount in the text and must be taken very seriously, the context in which they are worked out is not allegorical, still less abstract. The book's subject-matter is the education of girls. The biblical motto of Marcia Blaine's is 'O where shall I find a virtuous woman, for her price is above rubies' (p.6).

## Gender and Marcia Blaine's

## ACTIVITY

Spark's narrator is at great pains to 'place' Miss Brodie exactly among the Edinburgh spinsters of her period. Please now re-read pages 42–3 down to 'kirk services'. As an exercise, write down, as succinctly as possible, what Jean Brodie has in common with the 'legions of her kind' and what makes her different from many of them.

## DISCUSSION

She is solidly middle class in origin. She suffers from 'war-bereaved spinsterhood'. She experiments in what we now call 'life styles'. She is interested in the arts and takes a 'progressive' view of birth control. She is one of the 'great talkers and feminists' as distinct from the 'sober', church-going 'committee spinsters'. She is one of the 'progressive spinsters', and where she is exceptional is that she teaches in a 'traditional' school alongside 'orderly' spinsters.

Miss Brodie is pretty typical of a transitional phase of 'feminism', between the days of the militant suffragettes and the upsurge of the women's movement of the sixties. She talks 'to men as man-to-man'. But beside her male idols, *Il Duce* and the Führer, she sets before her pupils feminine role-models equally 'elect' – Thorndike and Pavlova. She tells her 'set' that they are 'all heroines in the making' (p.30).

## ACTIVITY

When we first meet them, all her special girls are already 'famous', though bathos deliciously attaches itself to the adjective. It is worth setting down the grounds of their fame as schoolgirls and noting what they 'become' in adult life. Has Jean Brodie successfully predestined their fates? You might try, as a useful exercise, making out your own list before reading mine.

Please re-read pages 62–3 from 'All that term' to 'Sandy who betrayed me'. What does it suggest about her view of women's 'roles' in life?

## DISCUSSION

The key word is 'dedication'. The exceptional woman must sacrifice herself to a 'vocation' of a dramatic kind. A missionary in the tropics is acceptable. A nun isn't. Pavlova studies her swans to perfect her 'dying swan' dance: 'That is true dedication.' By implication, we are to see Miss Brodie herself both as a kind of missionary and as a sort of artist.

As for the girls' fates:

Monica Douglas, 'famous mostly for mathematics ... and for her anger' is 'destined' to study science at university, not by Miss Brodie but by her own mathematical gifts. She marries a scientist, throws a live coal at his sister in one of her fits of anger, 'whereupon' he demands a separation. She is 'predestined' by her famous traits, but hardly by Miss Brodie, who despises science – 'jars and gases'.

Rose Stanley, 'famous for sex', is the vehicle of much irony at Miss Brodie's expense. Miss Brodie intends her to be a great lover, above the moral law. In fact it is her 'superficial' tomboy knowledge of 'trains, cranes, motor cars, Meccanos and other boys' affairs' (p.28) that makes her popular with her male contemporaries and gets her a reputation for 'sex'. She has 'no curiosity about sex at all' (p.88). Spark's narrator agrees with Miss Brodie that Rose has 'instinct', but she is not, as Miss Brodie supposes 'like a heroine from a novel by D.H. Lawrence'. She takes on her father's 'hard-headed and merry carnality' and makes 'a good marriage' to a 'successful businessman' soon after leaving school, 'shaking off Miss Brodie's influence as a dog shakes pond-water from its coat' (p.119).

Eunice Gardiner, 'famous for her spritely gymnastics and glamorous swimming', disappoints Miss Brodie with her 'commonplace ideas'. '…She wanted to be a Girl Guide, you remember. She was attracted to the Team Spirit' (p.126). She becomes a nurse and marries a doctor. She looks back with affection on Miss Brodie as 'full of culture … an Edinburgh Festival all on her own', as she sits, in middle age, placidly making a wool rug (pp.26–7).

Sandy Stranger, of course, becomes Sister Helena of the Transfiguration and author of a famous work of psychology. When we first meet her she is 'famous for her vowel sounds', which she has acquired from her English parents and by which Miss Brodie (snobbishly) is enraptured.

Jenny Gray is 'the prettiest and most graceful of the set' and this is 'her fame'. She decides to become an actress, and duly does so, despite Miss Brodie's telling her that she will 'never be a Fay Compton, far less a Sybil Thorndike' (p.126). So, self-destined, she emerges as 'an actress of moderate reputation' contentedly 'married to a theatrical manager' (pp.80–1).

Mary Macgregor's 'fame' rests on her 'being a silent lump', a useful scapegoat. Impressed by Brodie's propaganda, she wants to study classics. Miss Mackay allows her to take a little Latin, hoping that, out of gratitude, the girl will 'inform' her about Miss Brodie. 'But as the only reason that Mary had wanted to learn Latin was to please Miss Brodie', this ploy doesn't come off (p.77). Mary gets a mistaken impression that Latin and shorthand are the same thing, leaves school to become a shorthand typist, and, when she dies, is serving in the Wrens, 'clumsy and incompetent' as ever (p.15).

What pattern emerges from this? Miss Brodie's attempt (as Sandy sees it) to play the God of Calvin with her chosen elect, is a hopeless failure. Rose's 'instinct' leads her in an utterly conventional direction, Sandy's 'insight' into a 'vocation' that Miss Brodie abhors. Sandy does become a kind of 'heroine', sought after at her convent, but the fates of the rest of the set are unheroically disposed by what one might call 'predictable' conjunctions between their innate gifts and social pressures on them. Marriage, so far as we know, submerges Rose utterly. Mary *marries* a scientist – she does not, it seems, become one in her own right. Eunice marries a man from the profession which orders her own about. Even Jenny's acting career flourishes in marriage to one of the males who organize theatres and pay actresses. Mary cannot escape from her own unattractiveness and stupidity.

## ACTIVITY

Could you now please look in your Reader at the extracts from *On Literature as an Ideological Form* by Etienne Balibar and Pierre Macherey (pp.223–8). Which of their points have some implication for *MJB*, and why?

## DISCUSSION

You might have objected that a discussion centring on the role of the national education system in Republican France can hardly have much relevance to a non-state girl's school in Scotland. But three points that arise are at least worth arguing about.

(a) 'Literature is … an ensemble of language … inserted in a general schooling process so as to provide appropriate fictional effects, thereby reproducing bourgeois ideology'. Miss Brodie quotes poetry at her class with the implicit promise that it is liberating. But her own 'poetic' turns of phrase (as I will argue in the next subsection) are highly 'Edinburgh', very 'ideological' in Macherey's negative usage of that word.

(b) Literature is represented 'supremely as "style", as individual genius ... as something outside and above the process of education...'. This is very much how Brodie represents *all* the arts, and presents herself. Although she is ostensibly at odds with 'the process of education', as she claims, one could argue that in fact she furthers its role in 'reproducing bourgeois ideology'.

(c) Finally, literature-as-ideology works on the rule that 'thou shalt describe all forms of class struggle save that which determines thine own self'. Miss Brodie, 'literature' incarnate, sees John Knox versus Mary 'the gay French Queen', in the Old Town, but thinks little about the unemployed victims of the dominant class of which she is a hanger-on. Sandy recognizes the falsehood of Brodie's position.

I'll draw two further points from this discussion. Firstly, it is important to recognize, as a student considering fiction, poetry and drama, that the idea of 'literature' is highly problematic. What we like to think of as 'beautiful', 'noble' or 'critical' works may, in the context of 'education' where we meet them, be serving a process of ideological mystification and social repression – for instance, in privileging 'elegant' prose in Standard English over the actual speech forms of students and pupils from ordinary homes. *But*, secondly, surely it is an immense strength of Spark's novel that it is so acute in exploring how what claims to be 'liberating' in education – 'drawing out' – may in fact be repressive – 'putting in' –, and how 'literature' itself (Tennyson, Charlotte Brontë, Stevenson in Sandy's case) may simply generate fantasies reinforcing existing relations of class and gender? *MJB* works *against* 'literature-as-ideology'. It is implicitly critical even of its own fictional form.

However, Marcia Blaine's, I have suggested, is not a particularly repressive establishment. It doesn't need to be. Middle-class 'Edinburgh' is perfectly capable of pushing its girls into conventional lives, while buying polish, accomplishments and useful skills from a preferred educational establishment. 'Gender' is efficiently reproduced, despite Jean Brodie's fascinating behaviour in her middle-aged prime. Even Sandy chooses a respectable outlet for her unusual spirituality.

Middle-class 'Edinburgh', I think, also succeeds in installing its own prudish distaste for sexuality. You may find this remark surprising. Both Miss Brodie and Sandy have 'illicit' liaisons. Rose and Jenny make normal 'contented' marriages. A whole year of the Brodie set's life is characterized by obsessive interest in sex.

But consider the stand-off with which the novel opens. The 'Edinburgh' boys stand confronting the Marcia Blaine girls behind a 'protective fence of bicycles' which creates 'the impression that at any moment' the boys are 'likely to be away'. The Brodie set are first seen 'standing very close to each other because of the boys'.

Miss Brodie sleeps with the silly, retarded Lowther, it seems, out of a perverse feeling combining renunciation of Teddy and 'dedication' to the less attractive man. Sandy challenges Lloyd to make her his mistress because of a wish to cheat Miss Brodie and defy her God-playing – then opts for a life of celibacy. Jenny says she feels 'past' sex at the age of twelve. 'This', we are told, is 'strangely true' – her sense of 'erotic wonder' disappears until she is nearly forty (pp.80–1). The 'possibilities' of sex, so avidly explored by Jenny and Sandy in their 'research', aged eleven, have remained 'hidden'.

## *ACTIVITY*

What are we to make of the culmination of that 'sex laden year'? Please re-read, on pages 66–71, the episode concerning the man who 'joyfully' exposes himself to Jenny beside the river. This passage is rather puzzling. Why does Sandy feel so strongly that Miss Brodie must not be told?

## DISCUSSION

That Sandy should 'desert' Alan Breck and Mr Rochester to fall in love with a policewoman she has never seen seems a credible, if extreme, example of girlish calf-love for a heroine-figure (characterized only by her 'short, fair, curly hair' and her 'Morningside' pronunciation of 'nasty' as 'nesty', which upsets Sandy, famous for vowels). But how could telling Miss Brodie about the indecent exposure affect the 'undecided' state of her relationship with Mr Lowther? Is Sandy trying to shield her romantic teacher from unromantic truths, such as the fact that the male organ is like a 'fallen nestling' or 'strange plant'? How does this connect with the 'change in Rose', with Miss Brodie's blatant attempt to involve her with Teddy Lloyd, and Miss Brodie's 'unfinished quality'? Sandy's state of mind here is so enigmatic that, paradoxically, the fiction reads 'completely true'. By *not* employing omniscience to explain it clearly, Muriel Spark's narrator convinces us that it represents 'experience', unmediated, untampered with. I am clear at any rate what category of 'experience' is evoked in the episode overall. It is *repression*. Sandy represses consciousness of a 'nesty' incident. This may relate to the clinical coldness – Teddy Lloyd calls it 'unnatural' – that Sandy brings to her relationship with the painter. Her 'insight', a quality applauded by Miss Brodie, eschews 'instinct', eschews Deirdre's fertility or Rose's 'merry carnality'. Her 'insight' has a furtive, prurient tendency, and is leading towards the indignant logic which will 'put a stop' to Miss Brodie.

Sandy transforms her own aptitude for fantasy with an analytical tool, 'insight', achieving such 'insight' as psychologists have. She could have gone in a quite different direction. Her 'hidden possibilities', not hidden from us readers, include the potential to be a literary artist.

One public role in which women have achieved unqualified eminence – except in nursing and theatrical arts it is hard to think of another one – is the writing of prose fiction. But the status of female poets has never been secure. The most celebrated women poets in Britain during our century have been Edith Sitwell and Stevie Smith, both easily marginalized as 'eccentrics', and Sylvia Plath, who committed suicide in her early thirties (the reputation of women as poets will be discussed in Block 7). Spark started writing as an aspiring poet. Gender, it might be suggested, forced this supremely gifted artist into a role she mistrusted – that of best-selling novelist. *Miss Jean Brodie* is not only a work of fiction, it is 'about fiction'.

## Poetic justice: Spark, fiction and language

> I don't claim that my novels are truth – I claim that they are fiction out of which a kind of truth emerges. And I keep in my mind that what I am writing is fiction because I am interested in truth – absolute truth – and I don't pretend that what I am writing is more than an imaginative extension of the truth – something inventive.
>
> (Spark, quoted in Massie, 1979, p.11)

5.47 Spark's narrators are strong personalities. Sudden violence occurs often in her fiction, described in a matter-of-fact way, as if with relish. One reviewer asked: 'Why fabricate characters at whose expense you can then exercise your mercilessness?' Ruth Whittaker, quoting this, defends Spark: 'It is not so much that Mrs Spark deliberately invents characters simply in order to express her

contempt for them: rather that they embody her view of the fallen world'
(Whittaker, 1982, p.41). So Mary Macgregor, say, 'embodies' the sad fact that
some human beings lack intelligence, lack charm and are doomed to bad luck
– the 'nevertheless' principle?

*5.48*  I think that discomfort over Spark's 'merciless' moments is inseparable
from the pleasure her wit provides. Shock is involved in both cases. Language
in *MJB* constantly surprises us, teasingly:

(a)  *'Where there is no vision'*, Miss Brodie had assured them, *'the people perish.
     Eunice, come and do a somersault in order that we may have comic relief.'*
     (p.7)

(b)  Some days it seemed to Sandy that Miss Brodie's chest was flat, no bulges
     at all, but straight as her back. On other days *her chest was breast-shaped* and
     large, very noticeable...
     (p.11)

(c)  The story of *Miss Brodie's felled fiancé* was well on its way...
     (p.13)

(d)  ...they had embarked on a course of research which they called 'research'...
     (p.17)

These quotations are unmistakeably 'Sparkeian'. They are sharply funny.
Unlike characteristically 'Wodehouseian' phrasings, they go beyond
subverting clichés and generating comic figures of speech. There is a
(*nevertheless*) underlay of seriousness. In (a) there is a grotesque apposition of
Holy Writ (Proverbs 29:18) with 'comic relief', an apposition that points to
Miss Brodie's confusion of God's will with her own whim. Point (b) prepares
us to doubt the authority of Sandy's viewpoint. Are Miss Brodie's changes of
shape due to changes of dress? Or is it that Sandy's subjective viewpoint
imaginatively distorts ('transfigures') what is in front of her? Point (c) is
'mercilessly' dismissive, with its comic alliteration, of the tragic loss which,
according to Miss Brodie, has shadowed her life. Point (d) insists that we see
the study of sex by small girls as no less serious than scientific enquiry by
adults.

## ACTIVITY

There are four story-tellers in this book: Miss Brodie, Sandy, Sandy-and-Jenny,
and the narrator. Could you, without re-reading their tales, describe the styles
of the first three?

## DISCUSSION

Miss Brodie's tale of the 'felled fiancé', when one looks at it again, is more
businesslike than one remembered. Miss Brodie produces, on the whole, short,
down to earth statements, 'leavened' by 'poetical' clichés: 'He fell like an
autumn leaf ... Hugh was one of the Flowers of the Forest' (pp.12–13). It
seems more fulsome in the retelling (pp.71–2) when Hugh has become an
artist.

Sandy, at this stage, is 'fascinated by this method of making patterns with
facts' – Miss Brodie is 'making her new love story fit the old'. She admires
'the technique' despite feeling a 'pressing need to prove Miss Brodie guilty of
misconduct' (p.72). Her own fictionalizing gift has been perverted (I would
say) by 'Edinburgh' prudery.

We first encounter it as she works with Jenny on 'The Mountain Empire'. The language here is that of 'romantic' historical fiction (p.19). Her solo mental encounters with the Lady of Shalott (pp.21–2) and Stevenson's Alan Breck (pp.28–30) are closer to the sharpness of 'real' poetry, stilted phrases notwithstanding. Her identification of herself with Jane Eyre in conversation with Mr Rochester (p.58) shows her capacity, now she is rather older, to imitate a nineteenth-century style more closely.

Finally, Sandy falls into a mental style that corruptly, if hilariously, merges the jargon of Sunday newspaper police court reports with the discourse of romantic fiction. With Sergeant Anne Grey ('Angry') she forms a partnership dedicated 'to eliminate sex from Edinburgh and environs'. Though their mutual understanding is 'too deep for words' (p.69, a 'romantic' cliché), they apply grubby euphemisms – 'certain condition … liaison … described as singing master' – to the Brodie–Lowther relationship (pp.68–9). Sandy thinks of herself as *creating* (with Jenny) the 'incriminating documents' needed to bring Brodie to book. She is playing God here like Miss Brodie herself – and like a novelist. Fiction is impermissibly becoming confused with fact. However, within a few pages, Sandy and Jenny have renounced fiction: they hide the 'incriminating documents' forever. Fictionalizing is repressed along with memory of the man who exposed himself. From now on Sandy will seek knowledge non-fictionally, as a psychologist. But her last Brodie letter is a masterpiece in its way: discourses are bizarrely juxtaposed with wonderful comic effect. 'Intimacy' and 'misconduct', police-court euphemisms for 'sex', jut up among the romantic euphemisms: 'melted into each others arms', 'giving myself to you' and this wonderful mixture is followed by a close imitation of Miss Brodie's own conversational style (p.73). Edinburgh is the city, as Miss Brodie has pointed out to her pupils (p.33), both of the 'embittered' John Knox, from whom present-day sexual repressiveness stemmed, and of 'the gay French Queen', Mary. The 'last letter' encapsulates the 'Edinburgh' doubleness – romance and prudery.

Miss Brodie's frequent archaisms – 'forsooth' (p.12), 'the day draws late' (p.35), 'of noble mien' (p.23) – place her, early in the book, as an addict of chivalric fantasy, such as makes her declare: 'If I were to receive a proposal of marriage tomorrow from the Lord Lyon King of Arms, I would decline it' (p.23), implying that the custodian of Scotland's heraldic tradition must be seen as the most eligible man conceivable.

However, Miss Brodie's speech is also studded with routine 'Edinburgh' banalities. 'Speech is silver, silence is golden' (p.13), 'discretion is the better part of valour' (p.47), represent the values of daytime Deacon Brodies – the canny caution which complements 'Edinburgh' prudery. When she writes to Sandy after her dismissal, her tone combines the peevishness of outraged *propriety* with inane evocations of Soul, Beauty, Truth and Goodness (p.126).

She is in many respects *commonplace*. And if we grant that the 'transfiguration of the commonplace' occurs in this book, to whom do we attribute it? To Miss Brodie's eccentric methods, beauty 'in her prime' and flamboyant remarks? To Sandy's imagination? To Spark's narrator? Or to all three?

Is the 'glamour' associated with certain events at Marcia Blaine's and beyond simply an effect of fresh childhood vision? This is certainly the case with regard to the 'secret joy' with which Sandy visits the science room with its 'lawful glamour' (p.25). But by the time Sandy is admiring Teddy Lloyd's 'magical transfiguration' in painting all the set as different Jean Brodies, our sense of what is involved is complicated.

*ACTIVITY*

Please re-read the first two paragraphs on page 111. What is the salient idea here?

## DISCUSSION

Miss Brodie is compared to 'dark heavy Edinburgh' transfigured by a 'special pearly white light'. In her case, the light is provided by a sense of her 'folly'. It is her *silliness* which generates Sandy's affection for her. Lloyd, the artist, with the 'economy' that Sandy admires, has transfigured every sitter into the woman he 'loves'.

This objectifies Miss Brodie's own 'silly' solipsism (a solipsist sets herself or himself at the centre of everything and derives meaning in the universe only from her or his perception and consciousness); Miss Brodie has seen everyone – her set, Lloyd, Lowther – only in relation to her own personality in her prime. This allies with her sub-theological antinomianism. Yet Sandy finds the latter so dangerous that she must be stopped, the former 'silly' and therefore 'transfiguring'.

The 'nature of moral perception' is the subject of Sandy's 'odd psychological treatise' (p.35). It is troublesome for moralists that aesthetics and ethics get so muddled up. We find it hard to believe that people whom we perceive as beautiful might be wicked. Pig-eyed Sandy is a likelier villain than Miss Brodie with her Roman beauty. It is indeed hard to credit, on a fine day in Edinburgh, that this gracious city has been associated not just with 'Enlightenment' but also with a narrowness of spirit, which created, by reaction, Mr Hydes and Miss Brodies.

## ACTIVITY

Please, as a final exercise, look again at two passages: Sandy's birthday tea *à deux* with Jenny on pages 16–17, and the scene where Miss Brodie teaches on the lawn in springtime, page 71. How would you contrast the images of happiness conveyed?

## DISCUSSION

Sandy, even at this age, conceptualizes happiness. The 'unfamiliar pineapple' conveys a 'special happiness' different from 'the happiness of play' which one enjoys unawares. And this is sacred, 'nothing to do with eating' – she resents her mother's implication that 'the main idea of the party' has been the food. The pineapple is not 'commonplace', but Sandy – already 'religious' in tendency – deliberately 'transfigures' it. I would not call this passage 'poetic'.

The later one is. Human and inanimate entities are combined in a delicious vision of spring. Miss Brodie is moved by 'delight' to command her girls to listen to the song another teacher matches to the 'clip clop of the ponies', just as the 'grass, the sun and the birds' have lost 'their self-centred winter mood and [begun] to think of others'. Happiness is occurring: solipsism is momentarily defeated.

*5.49*   I would not trust whatever theories Sandy has about the psychology of moral perception. It is impossible to trust Miss Jean Brodie's perception of the world as transfigured by her own will and whim. I trust Spark's narrator, who executes what might be called 'poetic justice', who creates memorable images of a beautiful woman in her prime, which transfigure what is commonplace in her, and leave Sandy reiterating her conviction that (for good or ill?) Miss Brodie was the crucial influence on her young life.

*5.50*   Spark's Catholic position insists on human sinfulness in a fallen world. But 'poetic' perception can provide a fleeting sense of redemption, of grace widely, even generally, conferred – as the pearly sun redeems dark heavy Edinburgh.

# 6  O'Connor: 'Revelation'

*6.1*  In the first section of this block Cicely Havely established several ways in which literature and ideology are related to one another; the following story, 'Revelation', is a good illustration of one of her categories, 'religious ideology'. You will recall that she then went on to discuss Kipling's story 'A Sahibs' War', one of her aims being to 'disinter its ideological levels', a task that was, in the end, far from easy to complete with confidence. I am going to ask you to perform a similar exercise on the story that follows, 'Revelation', but as you now have some experience of what to look for in this kind of analysis, there will be no study guide. Instead, I shall give you certain starting points and then suggest you read the story through, making notes as you do so.

*6.2*  The first starting point I offer you is that this story has a powerful and unambiguous lesson to convey, and that in one sense its ideological position is crystal clear. I say 'in one sense' because, as we have seen, fiction often offers more than simply one point of view.

## *ACTIVITY*

Now please read the story (Prose Anthology pp.200–221). Hazard a guess (if you don't know already) at the sex, nationality and beliefs of the writer – information that will be revealed after you have formed your own impressions from the story.

Here are some points to bear in mind as you read:

(a)  What is the significance of the title?

(b)  What ideological issues does it raise? Can you think of a biblical quotation that sums up the ending?

(c)  What are we to make of Mrs Turpin – are we encouraged to judge her in any way?

(d)  How do irony and symbolism feature in the story?

(e)  Do you find the story funny? Is this part of Flannery O'Connor's intention?

Do not continue with this material until you have spent some time answering, or sketching notes for, questions (a) to (e) above. (What follows under 'Discussion' is meant only to be a quick answer to issues that will receive fuller consideration later.)

## *DISCUSSION*

(a)  'Revelation' could mean several things. In ordinary usage, it means a discovery, a perception. In a religious context, it takes on a more specific meaning: 'divine revelation' refers to a communication from God, whether through the Jewish prophets, members of the churches or, more specifically, the Bible. To quote from the introduction to the Revelation of St John in the Jerusalem Bible: 'The framework of a Revelation is always a vision of hidden supernatural events; the language in which the vision is described is richly symbolic and so allusive that the message can be interpreted in more ways than one.' Flannery O'Connor's story contains a number of references to religion, and Ruby Turpin is a 'church-going woman', so when we are told at the climax of the first part of the story in the waiting room that she 'held her breath, waiting as for a revelation', it is reasonable to assume that what she hears will be of some religious significance. According to the Oxford English Dictionary 'revelation' can also mean the disclosure of previously unknown facts about a person. All these meanings, I would argue, apply to this story, though perhaps the one that spans them all is the Revelation of St John, because the story is essentially about what theologians call eschatology – the ultimate fate of the universe, which, in Christian terms, means the Four Last Things at the end of time, Death, Judgement, Heaven and Hell. What Ruby Turpin sees for a brief moment in her vision in the hog pen is 'a vast horde of souls ... rumbling toward heaven', which in St John's terms is 'a new heaven and a new earth' (Revelation 21).

(b)  There are several ideological issues in this story and I shall be examining them in turn. For a start, the story is cast in specifically Christian terms with frequent reference to the person of Jesus, to being 'saved', and to an eternal destiny in heaven or hell. The quotation I had in mind was 'many will be first that were last, and last that were first' (Matthew 19:30). Then, within this general Christian understanding there are subtle variations between 'Bible-belt' Protestantism and a more specifically Catholic understanding of salvation. There is also the issue of racism and the various ways in which society is divided up by Mrs Turpin and others who think like her.

(c)  Ruby Turpin, like Jean Brodie, is a character not easily forgotten. The two women have, in fact, a certain amount in common: both want to dominate, are self-satisfied and completely convinced of the rectitude of their opinions, especially when it comes to judging other people. Fairly clearly, Ruby Turpin *is* judged in the closing paragraphs of the story and found wanting, but did you feel sympathy with her at any point in the story?

(d)  The point of this question was simply to alert you to how irony and symbolism feature in the writing. Do the pigs, for example, suffused 'with red glow', remind you of anything? Could they refer to the biblical Gadarene swine, into which Jesus sends the demonic spirits; and is the 'glow' perhaps an allusion to the flames of hell? And why does the colour of the sky keep changing? And why, in fact, *does* the revelation come to respectable Ruby Turpin? Is this meant to be a 'black joke' with a purpose?

(e)  I *hope* you found the story funny. I'm sure the author intended it be so: an audience to whom it was read (by a friend of the author's) shortly after its composition (1964) 'laughed until they cried' (O'Connor, 1979, p.563). But, as you have discovered with Muriel Spark's novel, this is not simply 'entertainment' of the kind P.G. Wodehouse set out to provide. Its intention could hardly be more serious. Does this make the author one with a purpose, a member of one of the groups listed by Cicely Havely in her introduction to this block? What conclusions did you draw about the author? The author was, in fact, a white Roman Catholic woman from the Southern States of the US. Flannery O'Connor (christened Mary Flannery O'Connor), who lived most of her relatively short life in Georgia, died at the age of 39 from lupus, a disease that she contracted at the age of 25. You might, I think, have got some of these facts: that she was female, from the South, white and, perhaps, a Roman Catholic. I say 'perhaps' to this last because one question I want to consider is whether a Catholic reader will spot aspects of the story that might not be immediately obvious to non-Catholic readers. Is there a 'code' in the story, and one that might be evident only to a particular 'interpretive community', to take up Stanley Fish's term introduced in Block 3?

*6.3* It becomes evident fairly early in the story that this is no ordinary tale of country folk. What, for example, is going on when the 'ugly girl' reading a book called *Human Development* starts giving Mrs Turpin stares from her blue eyes, which 'appeared alternately to smoulder and blaze' and which 'seemed lit all of a sudden with a peculiar light, an unnatural light'? These are signals, I suggest, that this story is not simply to be taken in terms of its own narrative, that the author is hinting at a level of meaning over and above 'what happens'. With this in mind, let me go back to an earlier point in the story when the conversation between the 'stylish lady' (in fact, the ugly girl's mother) and Mrs Turpin has moved from the subject of body weight and diets to 'disposition':

> 'Well, as long as you have such a good disposition,' the stylish lady said, 'I don't think it makes a bit of difference what size you are. You just can't beat a good disposition.'
>
> (p.202)

The way the stylish lady is using the term, it means simply being 'good-natured', and this is something on which Mrs Turpin particularly prides herself:

> 'I thank the Lord he has blessed me with a good one', Mrs Turpin said. 'The day has never dawned that I couldn't find something to laugh at.'
>
> (p.210)

## ACTIVITY

One of the ironies I hinted at earlier is that we learn later that her husband Claud sees another side of her and 'paid no attention to her humours' (i.e. bad tempers). There is no doubt that the term 'good disposition' is being used in this day-to-day sense, but to a Catholic reader it has another, much deeper resonance: to receive the Sacraments with a good disposition means to be in a state of grace, to be in a state of friendship with God and this, we later discover, is just what Mrs Turpin is not. If you accept this point, what do you make of the ugly girl?

## DISCUSSION

She's really rather a puzzle. Both ugly and bad-tempered, she is given the name of Mary Grace, and there surely has to be significance in this choice. 'Mary' is the name of the mother of Christ, and 'Grace' also has a theological significance, suggesting, in various forms and to put it at its simplest, the presence of God. (The Oxford English Dictionary defines it as 'the free and unmerited favour of God', the 'divine influence which operates in men to regenerate and sanctify, and to impart strength to endure trial and resist temptation'.) But if the ugly girl in some way represents God, why is she both disfigured and badly behaved? Is the author suggesting, perhaps, that appearances are deceptive, that what seems ugly to Mrs Turpin might not be to God? The answer is related, I think, to the boy in the waiting room, who, according to his mother, 'Took sick and turned good': he improved in his behaviour as a result of his illness. It is a theological point about the relationship of suffering to spiritual development, one that may have had a particular meaning to Flannery O'Connor, who wrote this story in the last year of her life. Suffering is part of what theologians call the 'economy of salvation': Jesus, the 'Lamb of God', took the sin of the world upon himself. His followers are asked to share that burden and to see through the suffering to the Resurrection. (O'Connor had in fact gone on a pilgrimage to Lourdes with her mother in 1958 and, according to one of her friends, 'dreaded the possibility of a miracle' (Fitzgerald, 1965, p.xxiv), not because she loved her illness but, presumably, because she had learned to cope with it and to make use of it in her spiritual life.) The author herself admitted that, while she had met many a Mrs Turpin in real life, Mary Grace was perhaps the result of reading a number of theology books. And the title of the book she is reading – *Human Development* – must also be related to the Christian teaching on the fall and redemption of humankind. Behind this apparently simple story is the history of the human race as understood by orthodox Christianity – which is that after the fall from grace represented by the story of Adam's disobedience, all had to be remade by and in Christ.

This thinking is the theological backbone to 'Revelation' which, while radical and uncompromising, is entirely orthodox. These ideas will be familiar to you if you have some knowledge of Christian theology. If this is not your position, then it may take longer for you to reach a satisfactory understanding of Flannery O'Connor's purposes. But let us start be establishing just *what happens* in the story.

## ACTIVITY

Describe in a paragraph the essential points of the narrative.

## DISCUSSION

The bare bones of the story are simply exposed: Ruby Turpin visits her doctor with her husband. In the waiting-room she feels herself being stared at by an ugly girl who eventually attacks her physically and gives her a 'message', telling her to go back to hell. She and her husband return home. While he goes off to take the 'Negroes' home, she goes to sluice down the hog pen and, reflecting on the events of the day, feels anger welling up in her: she confronts God with her charge, argues with him, and receives in response a strange vision of the blessed entering the Kingdom of Heaven, with people like herself coming last.

So, it now seems that the 'revelation' comes in several forms: firstly to Mrs Turpin in the waiting-room when, after the attack, she 'held her breath, waiting, as for a revelation', and then right at the end of the story where she has a 'visionary light' in her eyes. The *meaning* of the revelation is another matter. Flannery O'Connor makes the reader cautious about establishing meaning, for she once said:

> The meaning in a story cannot be paraphrased and if it's there it's there, almost more as a physical than an intellectual fact.
>
> (quoted in Alther, 1980, p.6)

What she meant by this, I think, is that a text is unique and possesses a quality that is to be appreciated only on its own terms. Nevertheless, students of literature need to probe a little more closely into what the text is saying.

## ACTIVITY

At the beginning of this section, I stated that this text has an unambiguous 'message'. How would you sum it up?

## DISCUSSION

It is really a parable, I would argue, for the virtuous and the complacent. Most striking to me is that sentence in the penultimate paragraph, in the midst of Ruby Turpin's vision:

And bringing up the end of the procession was a tribe of people whom she recognized at once as those who, like herself and Claud, had always had a little of everything and the God-given wit to use it right. She leaned forward to observe them closer. They were marching behind the others with great dignity, accountable as they had always been for good order and common sense and respectable behaviour. They alone were on key. Yet she could see by their shocked and altered faces that even their virtues were being burned away.

(p.220)

If you agree with me that this story has a parable quality to it, what lesson, or lessons, can be drawn from it? Behind this story, I feel, is the account in the New Testament of the Pharisee and the tax-gatherer who go to the Temple to pray (Luke 18): the Pharisee recounts his virtues to God; the tax-gatherer pleads for mercy as a sinful man, and it is the second prayer that is acceptable. Ruby Turpin is a modern day Pharisee: she is complacent and considers herself virtuous. The important point is that she (and those like her) do receive the salvation they hope for (and the story ends on a joyful note with the blessed souls 'shouting hallelujah') but, in God's eyes, their scale of values is back to front and all the people they despise will enter first.

## ACTIVITY

How does the author build up Ruby Turpin's character, and how are we encouraged to see her?

## DISCUSSION

First impressions of Ruby Turpin are not very favourable: she has 'little bright black eyes', with which she quickly sums up the situation in the waiting-room which she immediately begins to dominate, ordering her husband around and addressing the room at large. The first part of the story is seen through her eyes: in the terms used by Dorrit Cohn in Block 3, this is 'psycho-narration' of a 'consonant' kind (the narrator is not distanced from the character), and as she looks around, she forms a judgement on everyone in the waiting-room, deciding, significantly, to make an ally of the 'stylish lady' while dismissing practically everyone else, especially the acned girl and 'white-trashy' mother. This leads her on to the game she plays at night, debating with herself who she would choose to be if she couldn't be herself. Her total failure to understand the uniqueness of human identity and the dignity of others' lives is summed up in her final decision that, if she couldn't be herself, she would be 'a neat clean respectable Negro woman, herself but black'. This develops into her wider social classification of Southern society, but when the complexity of the task of fitting everyone into her system gets too great, she solves the problem by shipping everyone off to death in a gas-oven. This horrific, fascistic solution is an index not only of her small-mindedness but also of her lack of love for her fellow human beings.

In the next part of the story, Ruby Turpin is at pains to establish her place in the social hierarchy by describing her and her husband's property, and this introduces the hog theme through the confrontation with the 'white-trash woman'. The entry of the black boy takes the conversation on to the place of blacks in Southern society, which gives the 'pleasant lady' and Mrs Turpin the chance to be patronizing. The song on the radio leads Mrs Turpin into another bout of self-congratulation on her philanthropy and contentment with her lot, again seen in religious terms, until it is rudely interrupted by the girl's attack on her.

Later, at home, Mrs Turpin thinks over what the girl said to her and wonders why she was chosen for this message:

> She had been singled out for the message, though there was trash in the room to whom it might justly have been applied ... the message had been given to Ruby Turpin, a respectable, hard-working, church-going woman. The tears dried. Her eyes began to burn instead with wrath.
>
> (p.214)

Mrs Turpin can't bring herself to tell her husband the contents of the message, though she does eventually tell the 'negro' women, only to find her rage increased by their excessively flattering responses. At the climax of the story, she is described as having 'the look of a woman going single-handed, weaponless, into battle', and the person she is confronting is, of course, God – which makes the situation both comic and awesome. She then goes back to 'the game', sarcastically asking God why she was made the way she was if her life is not pleasing to him. At the height of her fury, she shouts at God, asking him: 'Who do you think you are?' She gets a reply in the form of the vision in which the 'white trash', the 'niggers', the 'freaks', are all before her in the 'vast horde of souls rumbling towards Heaven'. God, it seems, *does* prefer these people she despises so much. What point is the author making here? Should we feel any sympathy for Ruby Turpin? Her first name calls to mind the Old Testament sentiment that a virtuous woman has a price above rubies (as you may remember from the motto of the Marcia Blaine school in *The Prime of Miss Jean Brodie*), though the second is reminiscent, perhaps, of 'turpitude'.

One point, surely, is that while it is good to be virtuous, this is worthless if it is not informed by love, but is accompanied instead by judgemental, dismissive, self-satisfied attitudes. In spite of her continual references to Jesus, Ruby Turpin seems to have a far from Christian disposition as traditionally understood. Another point is that Ruby Turpin wants God on her terms – 'Who do you think you are?' is surely one of the funniest questions in any of the texts in this course? She gets her reply in no uncertain terms in the form of the vision, her 'revelation' that God loves all his creation and that before his absolute being no one is justified by actions or virtues – indeed, these must be 'burned away' by purgatorial fire because they obstruct and focus attention on the self. Purgatory in Catholic teaching is a transitional stage of preparation between death and entering the Kingdom of Heaven. This is the 'field of living fire' that Ruby Turpin sees in her vision. Further, God is free to reward whom he likes and in whatever manner: Ruby Turpin and those like her who want to exercise control over their own and other people's lives are, in effect, attempting to usurp this freedom. What she says on her own behalf is not untrue – she has the virtues of hard work and an orderly life, and it is possible to share her indignation at the slothful characters she describes. But I don't think we are expected to feel much pity for her, except in the sense that she has to learn an important lesson in a painful manner. All the same, Flannery O'Connor liked her character, as she remarked in a letter on the 16 May 1964:

> I like Mrs Turpin as well as Mary Grace. You got to be a very big woman to shout at the Lord across a hog pen. She's a country female Jacob.
>
> (O'Connor, 1979, p.577)

The narrative methods of 'consonant psycho-narration' and 'quoted monologue' enable the author to stay close to her character and show the working of her misguided mind.

# Mary Grace

## ACTIVITY

Mary Grace is the other major character in the story. How does she differ from the other characters in 'Revelation' and what is her function in the story? Why do you think Flannery O'Connor liked her?

## DISCUSSION

From the beginning she is marked out as someone singular. She is fat and ugly, and is described as reading a 'blue book' entitled *Human Development*. (Why blue? Perhaps because blue is associated with heaven, and it is considered the Virgin Mary's colour?) She displays intense animosity towards Mrs Turpin from the start, in contrast to the latter's laughter and evidence of her 'good disposition'. Her most remarkable features are eyes which 'appeared alternately to smoulder and to blaze'. (Eyes are carefully described throughout the story – could this be because they are said to be the 'windows of the soul'?) Then we are given a hint that in some way she is 'different' from the other people in the waiting-room – when she slams her books shut, her eyes 'seemed lit all of a sudden with a peculiar light, an unnatural light'. The 'unnatural' theme is taken up a little later when the girl pulls ugly faces at Mrs Turpin:

> She was looking at her as if she had known and disliked her all her life – all of Mrs Turpin's life, it seemed too, not just all the girl's life.
>
> (p.207)

As the girl is eighteen and Mrs Turpin is forty-seven, this removes her from the space–time continuum inhabited by all the other characters. She becomes a figure from another world with, it seems, a mission: fixing her eyes 'like two drills' on Mrs Turpin, it becomes evident to her victim that 'there was something urgent behind them'. As well as being ugly, it seems that Mary Grace is also an ungrateful daughter 'who just criticizes and complains all day long'. When she attacks Mrs Turpin, particular emphasis is put again on her eyes which, now that pent-up feelings are released, 'seemed a much lighter blue than before, as if a door that had been tightly closed behind them was now open to admit light and air' (p.212). Then the earlier hint that she is unlike the other people in the room is spelled out:

> There was no doubt in her mind that the girl did know her, knew her in some intense and personal way, beyond time and place and condition.
>
> (p.212)

Once her message is delivered to Mrs Turpin, her part in the story is over and we hear no more of her. In allegorical terms her work is done – grace, in Christian theology, works on, and redeems, fallen nature. Here Mary Grace has 'worked' on Ruby Turpin. What are we to make of her 'otherworldliness'? Is she perhaps a messenger from God with a warning for Mrs Turpin? And why is she made so ugly? When an early reader of the story gave as the reason 'because Flannery loves her', she was described by the author as a 'very perceptive girl' (O'Connor, 1979, p.578). What is it in the character she liked, for on the face of it she is ugly and violent? I think it has to be, that, in contrast to Mrs Turpin, Mary Grace knows her own wounded state, and as a truthful person recognizes the hypocrisy and self-satisfaction of others. In a sense she is a freak, and freaks occur quite frequently in Flannery O'Connor's writing, usually as characters who, just because they stand out from their fellows, can convey truth too large to be contained within an 'ordinary discourse'. As the author herself once said, 'To be able to recognize a freak, you have to have some conception of the whole man' – in other words, fallen humanity made whole again through the redemptive love of Christ. On another occasion she put the same point slightly differently, setting the quotidian against the eternal:

> A view taken in the light of the absolute will include a good deal more than one taken merely in the light provided by a house-to-house survey.

By 'the absolute', she means that the religiously-minded, like herself, see all life in terms of absolute values, everything leading to God the creator and his plan for his creation. She was well aware, however, that her own views were not those of most people around her. As she wrote to a friend,

> I believe too that there is only one Reality and that that is the end of it, but the term, 'Christian Realism' has become necessary for me, perhaps, in a purely academic way, because I find myself in a world where everyone has his compartment, puts you in yours, shuts the door and departs. One of the awful things about writing when you are a Christian is that for you the ultimate reality is the Incarnation, the present reality is the Incarnation, and nobody believes in the Incarnation; that is, nobody in your audience. My audience are the people who think God is dead.
>
> (O'Connor, 1979, p.92)

6.4   Let us now look more specifically at the effect of Flannery O'Connor's religious commitment on her work.

## Religion and 'Revelation'

6.5   Let me take up one of Cicely Havely's questions in the introductory section of this block: was Flannery O'Connor writing with a purpose? Did she hope to convert people to Christianity by her writing? There is no simple answer to this question. She certainly saw her writing as a vocation, and the nature of it indicates that she wanted to present, through her fiction, the immensity of the belief she was raised in and remained faithful to until her death. As she wrote to a friend:

> I write the way I do because (not though) I am a Catholic. That is a fact and nothing covers it like the bald statement.
>
> (O'Connor, 1979, p.90)

And as she conceded in an interview:

> I will admit to certain preoccupations with belief and with death and grace and the devil.
>
> (Ross, 1963, p.33)

She certainly saw the writer's task as that of the prophet:

> There is the prophetic sense of 'seeing through' reality and there is also the prophetic function of recalling people to known but ignored truths.
>
> (Wells, 1962, p.72)

6.6 I suggested earlier that a Catholic 'interpretive community' might see some things in the story that someone outside it would miss, yet apart from the Marian connection I have suggested, there is little in the story that any members of the mainstream Christian churches would have difficulty identifying with, and in this sense Flannery O'Connor is quite ecumenical in her outlook. But does the reader have to share her beliefs either to *understand* the story, or to like it?

## DISCUSSION

I don't think there can be any doubt that a reader needs a knowledge of basic Christian theology in order to understand the meaning of the story. Jesus is mentioned often in 'Revelation' and Ruby Turpin refers to how he has made her what she is. Flannery O'Connor once remarked rather sharply that 'while the South is hardly Christ-centred, it is most certainly Christ-haunted'. For this to make sense, you need to know that, in orthodox Christianity, God the Father is believed to have created all things through his Son, the second person in the Blessed Trinity. Similarly, Mrs Turpin's vision at the end of the story is one of salvation, the gathering of the blessed in the coming of the Kingdom. Unless you understand this view of 'reality' the story won't make a lot of sense. Whether you share those views is another matter. The story surely has to mean more to a reader who does than to one who doesn't? For a non-believing reader, the whole foundation of the story can only be myth, which would put it, perhaps, on the same plane as science fiction, a form of writing enjoyed by many who don't actually believe literally in what they read.

Another question in the introduction to this block asked whether literature 'perpetuates illusions'. A reader hostile to Flannery O'Connor's beliefs might say that this is precisely what the story does. But your response surely depends upon your starting point.

## ACTIVITY

Can you, for a moment, try imagining how you think a committed Marxist might read the story?

## DISCUSSION

The whole Christian framework would, I think, be seen only as an illusion by a Marxist and, possibly, as a way of perpetuating social inequality by promising justice in an afterlife, rather than trying to improve society here and now. More probably, a Marxist critic would be interested in the economic divisions in the Southern state which is the location for the story. The distinctions made by Ruby Turpin – coloured people, white-trash, home-owners, home-and-land-owners, richer home-and-land-owners – reflect real divisions and represent a whole school of thinking in the Old South after the Civil War. Because Marxist critics are concerned with class-struggle and capitalist economies, it is probable that the exploitation of black labour by the Turpins on their farm would also be an area of the story on which to focus.

Pursuing this line of 'different readers', what about the gender of the reader? Will women read this story differently from men? The author herself did not think in these terms. Flannery O'Connor wants to transcend the concerns of gender and the attribution of qualities or lack of them to people on its basis. She once remarked:

> I just never think of ... qualities which are specifically feminine or masculine. I suppose I divide people into two classes: the Irksome and the non-Irksome, without regard to sex.
>
> (quoted in Alther, 1980, p.6)

Nevertheless, people and characters do possess gender, a fact that we are perhaps more inclined to explore in the 1990s than was the case in 1964 when 'Revelation' was written. How do the issues of gender and race feature in your thinking about the story? I don't want to go into these issues in great depth, but for me they focus on the three main people in the story – Ruby Turpin, Mary Grace, and God, two of them women and the third beyond gender.

Mrs Turpin is a dominant, strong woman: she lays a 'firm hand' on her husband's shoulder, *commands* him to kiss her, and, finally, shouts at God from the hog pen. Mary Grace, with her acned ugliness and violent behaviour, is hardly the embodiment of femininity as traditionally understood, while the 'white-trash' woman is deliberately made unattractive. In fact, none of the women in the story is very likeable: are the competitiveness between them in the waiting-room conversation, and then the crude flattery offered by the cotton-pickers to Mrs Turpin, examples of stereotypical 'women's behaviour'? The same question could be asked with regard to the portrayal of the 'negro workers' in the story. God, who does not appear directly in the story, is neither male nor female, though in his role as Father and Creator he takes a masculine identity, as we saw earlier. In the vision of the Kingdom of Heaven that concludes the story, people are referred to simply as 'souls', since in Christian teaching, though men remain men and women remain women, they are all made one in Christ (in St Paul's words: 'there are no more distinctions between … male and female, but all of you are one in Christ Jesus', Galatians 3:28–9. But life on earth, as the story shows, is far from this harmonious vision, and I want to turn now to its geographical location and associated 'regional' qualities.

## 'Revelation' and regionalism

*6.7*  The marked 'regional' qualities of Flannery O'Connor's story hardly need spelling out: there is the gospel music playing on the radio; some of the characters (noticeably the blacks and 'white-trash') speak in dialects; part of the agriculture is growing cotton; racist attitudes abound in obvious and less obvious ways. All these features mark this as a story set in the deep South of the United States. Does this make Flannery O'Connor a 'regional' writer? To a certain extent, the answer to this has to be 'yes', because, although she travelled (and lived for a while in New York), Flannery O'Connor spent most of her life (and her last years) in what was known as the 'Old South'. As one US critic put it:

> Miss O'Connor never made blacks the central figures in her stories. Nor, really, did she get into the heads of Yankees, either. She knew which 'social scene' was hers: not the upper-class South; not really, with a few exceptions, its professional and business cadres; but overwhelmingly, its 'poor white' rural and smalltown folk, or its ordinary working-class men and women, some of whom, admittedly, do have their higher aspirations.
>
> (Coles, 1980, pp.4–5)

*6.8*  And, as Coles observes elsewhere, Flannery O'Connor kept to her 'own side' of the racial divide. In fact, the 1960s were a time of great events in the South as desegregation got under way, but this was towards the end of Flannery O'Connor's life and, as Coles reports of a conversation between her, himself and his wife:

> She warned us not to become so caught up in a region's special (and then urgent) difficulties that we lost sight of what she referred to the several times we spoke, as 'the larger human drama in which we all of us have our parts to play'.
>
> (Ibid., p.xiv)

*6.9* So, racism is not the issue that she chooses to tackle in any way in her fiction, any more than gender: her principal concerns, both in this story and more generally, are what, for her, are the wider issues of redemption and salvation, unrelated to any specific group. It is because of this that she did not consider that being a 'Southern' writer had any primary, determining influence on her work. As she once commented:

> As a fiction writer who is a Southerner, I use the idiom and the manners of the country I know, but I don't consider that I write *about* the South.

(quoted in Fitzgerald and Fitzgerald, 1970, p.142)

*6.10* In fact, there *was* a group of Southern writers, known as the Agrarians, who opposed the growth of industrialism and advocated a return to a more traditional way of life. To some extent, Flannery O'Connor could be seen as part of this group but she escapes this categorization in the end for one simple reason – her Catholicism. As she herself remarked:

> The only thing that keeps me from being a regional writer is being a Catholic, and the only thing that keeps me from being a Catholic writer (in the narrow sense) is being a Southerner.

(quoted in Alther, 1980, p.5)

It was a somewhat unusual position to be a Catholic in the 'Bible-belt' South and it is just this conjunction that gives her the perspective to write so incisively and sharply about Southern society and its religious expressions. As she observed in a lecture, 'The Catholic novelist in the Protestant South', given the year before she died (later reprinted in *Mystery and Manners*):

> The South is traditionally hostile to outsiders except on her own terms ... The things that bind us together as Catholics are known only to ourselves. A secular society understands us less and less. It becomes more and more difficult in America to make belief believable, but in this the Southern writer has the greatest possible advantage. He lives in the Bible Belt ... in the South the Bible is known by the ignorant as well [as the educated], and it is always that *mythos* the poor hold in common that is most valuable to the fiction writer. When the poor hold sacred history in common, they have ties to the universal and the holy which allows the meaning of their every action to be heightened and seen under the aspect of eternity.

(O'Connor, 1972, pp.200–3)

*6.11* Flannery O'Connor's Catholicism links her to the author of the text in the previous section, Muriel Spark, for they share the same faith. *Revelation* is really the more optimistic text, describing the Beatific Vision of the Blessed in contrast to the harsh Calvinism portrayed and condemned in *The Prime of Miss Jean Brodie*, with its belief in the possibility of predestined damnation.

## Conclusion

*6.12* The theme of Block 4 is 'Literature and Ideology', and the running question throughout this part of the course is how far our beliefs and assumptions (whether or not consciously held) shape our perception and understanding of what we read. It is now time for a personal admission: I was asked to write on this text because I share Flannery O'Connor's Catholicism and consequently her understanding of the world we live in and the future we can expect. How do you think this has affected the way I have written about this text? Open University academics usually try to keep themselves largely out of the picture when writing course material, but in this case, given the theme of the block, that was not easy to do, as Angus Calder found in writing about *The Prime of Miss Jean Brodie*. Try asking yourself how you would write about 'Revelation' in, say, a TMA.

*6.13* It is clear, I think, that I admire this text greatly and consider it deeply funny, profound in its insight and beautifully written – 'crafted', it would be fair to say. But how would someone who does not share my beliefs read it? To illustrate the diversity of responses a text can produce, I am going to end with a paragraph from another member of the course team, Richard Allen who may, perhaps, reveal in the process his own 'ideological position'.

## 'Revelation': another perspective

*6.14* When I first read 'Revelation' I knew only that Flannery O'Connor was a woman who had lived in the southern states of the USA. The story impressed me, but my sense of its ideology was based on my own secular viewpoint and therefore differed from that discussed so far by Roger Day; I hope that reflecting on the difference between our readings will encourage you to define *your* sense of the ideology of the story.

*6.15* For me, the crucial element is not the references to religious motifs and topics but the representation of discrimination. It is this that seems to me to have the most extended treatment in the story. I use the word here not just in the familiar sense of 'discriminating against someone', i.e. acting against someone from prejudice, but also in the sense of 'discriminating between one thing/person and another', i.e. marking differences. The use of a doctor's waiting-room as the main setting is appropriate because people arrive there almost haphazardly, but are required to fall into an order to see the doctor. O'Connor focuses on the perception of Mrs Turpin, and uses her to show how discrimination is the key process in this society. Mrs Turpin immediately begins to sort those present into a hierarchy, first in simple terms – a child should give way to a woman – then in more complex ways. The story asks how we should order the 'gray-haired lady', the girl with the book and acne, the woman in the print-dress... The enclosure of the reader within Mrs Turpin's point of view makes it difficult for the reader to reject this activity of discriminating, which is fundamental to the society depicted ('Mrs Turpin occupied herself at night naming the classes of people'), without rejecting the story.

*6.16* That discrimination is fundamental to this society is shown by the way religion is affected; Jesus is seen by Mrs Turpin as the great assigner of places and originator of difference – 'You can either be a nigger or white-trash'. But the structure is also extended to include class difference as well as that based on property-ownership, appearance and, of course, race. The story asks how one places 'white-trash', the 'nigger', the 'ugly'. These issues, raised in Mrs Turpin's mind early in the story, are then developed and paralleled in the final scenes, on the farm with the black farm-hands. Each individual clearly knows the place they deserve or to which they are confined. Yet the story also exposes the falseness of the situation and the relationship of black and white in the hollowness of the dialogue. The black voice utters sycophantic cliché: 'You the sweetest lady I know', while the white voice thinks abruptly: 'You could never say anything intelligent to a nigger.'

*6.17* The story contains a high proportion of women characters and this prompted me to consider whether the story focused equally on gender difference and the relationships between women or women and men. To some extent this does seem so. The story represents female–male relationships as composed of a minimal amount of caring in the woman and a minimal amount of mutual support on the farm. Individual isolation again seems the key-note. The women, especially Mrs Turpin, are represented as strong, but there is no sense that O'Connor wants to pursue the idea that – as some feminists argue – all women are 'sisters under the skin'. Indeed the story focuses on the attack of one woman on another.

*6.18*   Mary Grace's attack is presented as unmotivated and irrational. On a realistic level, the most one could say is that the girl is annoyed by Mrs Turpin's sanctimonious utterances ('Thank you, Jesus, for making everything the way it is!'), but such an interpretation strains against the way O'Connor suddenly projects the reader into the attack. I feel prompted, then, to search for an interpretation which would cast the event in a more symbolic light, or see it as a part of the narrative strategy of the story. Perhaps, then, the attack illuminates the nature and consequences of difference and discrimination. This process, the narrative demonstrates, leads not to order but to violence. In the story, the attack is explicitly described as carrying a message to Mrs Turpin, but one that poses a problem for her and for the reader. The 'revelation' of the title is that the voice that appears to be able to order and control is inextricably part of the process she describes. Is the reader manoeuvred into a similar position? In the case of Mrs Turpin the situation is expressed through the contrast of her own pleasure at having 'all I got, a little of everything' and the horrifying thought that she is a 'wart-hog from hell'.

*6.19*   How, then, do I see religion figuring in the story? It is a part of the Southern culture described in the story, religious terms form part of the language and are used as names in a relatively 'natural' way, losing much of their significance in the process. As the story progresses religion takes on a different meaning: Mrs Turpin is referred to as being protected 'by divine Providence', voiced through the old black woman, and in the final vision there is 'a vast swinging bridge extending upward through a field of living fire. Upon it a vast horde of souls were rumbling towards heaven...' The narrative structure seems to press me into reading this as a way of solving the problem of individual isolation confronted in the story. Furthermore, for me the religious rhetoric of unity and transcendence is reinforced by echoes of European images from secular sources – the rainbow at the end of Lawrence's novel *The Rainbow*, or the rainbow bridge to Valhalla found in German myths. In this final vision or 'revelation', the differences dramatized earlier are dissolved: the 'white-trash' are now clean, the black people wear 'white robes'. The story ends on a rhetorical Utopian vision of 'souls climbing upward into the starry field and shouting hallelujah' (p.221), but this final comfort is only extended to the reader in the very last sentence, a more disturbing revelation is contained in the previous paragraph which undercuts the joy of the 'vast horde of souls'. For if opposites and discriminations are dissolved, then this process must be extended to Mrs Turpin and those like her who have 'a little of everything and the God-given wit to use it right' (p.220). Logic demands that 'virtues' (however questionable) are 'burned away'. A religious perspective might see this as the sort of constructive destruction found in the Book of Revelation. My secular viewpoint sees the process as a general merging into an amoral *mélange*.

*6.20*   The tensions within the ending seem to me to underline the story as a whole. It has a power firstly as a representation of a society in which discrimination is the dominant process compelling the individual into isolation and secondly through its depiction of the violent and extreme behaviour which exists in society. As a reader I may only perceive discrimination as a process which breaks down society – no representation of communal resistance is allowed. The reader is left to weigh the consequences of this world, perhaps – and in doing so to negotiate a way through the surprises of the story. In the final paragraph there is, as I have said, a vision of some kind of idealized transcendent world; earlier there is the savage attack of one person on another. Here again the story offers no explanation in human or social terms and the narrative refuses even a more literal symbolic interpretation. The scientific study of 'human development' – the title of Mary Grace's book – is thrown at the embodiment of religious prejudice, but the reader is left in a curious limbo unable to confront this question.

# 7  Lorca: 'Yerma'

## A note on Sections 7 and 8

The two plays which are the final case-studies in this block are studied from different points of view. Keith Whitlock has concentrated on the language of *Yerma* – or rather its languages, for he repeatedly draws your attention to its variety of dramatic 'signs' (which you will remember from your study of Esslin and Beckett's *Endgame* in Block 1). In his study of *The Island* on the other hand, Dennis Walder has concentrated on the highly political circumstances of the play's production. But as you will realize, both procedures are appropriate for both plays. Enough is indicated of the political circumstances of *Yerma*'s first production for you to understand why it was such a momentous event; and you have by now studied enough texts in detail to be able to analyse the 'languages' of *The Island*.

## Background

*7.1*   Federico García Lorca was born in 1898. His grandfather was a farmer who had grown wealthy on the *vega*, the rich agricultural land to the west of Granada, where the playwright grew up, and where (according to Ian Gibson, Lorca's biographer) 'no linguistic and few social distinctions separated wealthy and poor, peasants and landowners' (Gibson, 1983, pp.15–16). He studied in Granada, enjoying the city's rich intellectual life, and first achieved fame as a poet, though he was a talented artist and pianist too. His earliest theatrical attempts were with puppet plays and traditional farce; but his most successful theatrical work of the twenties, *Mariana Pineda*, first performed in 1927, dealt with Granada's nineteenth-century folk heroine and martyr to the cause of political freedom.

*7.2*   He resisted political classification, but his sympathies were clear enough in 1931 for him to be appointed director of a travelling theatre company, La Barraca, sponsored by the Ministry of Education in Manuel Azaña's newly elected Republican government, and dedicated to bringing the theatre to the people. Under his direction the group performed Spanish plays in the squares and market-places of villages all over the country, and the experience convinced him that the theatre could be revitalized and popular, as well as contributing to the three folk-tragedies that are his greatest dramatic work: *Blood Wedding* (1933), *Yerma* (1934) and *The House of Bernarda Alba* (1936). He was shot by Nationalist partisans at the outset of the Spanish Civil War in 1936.

*7.3*   Though the Second Republic was established in 1931, a right-wing coalition was in power when *Yerma* was first produced in December 1934, so the struggle between the progressive Republicans and the traditionalist Nationalists was moving inexorably towards the war that erupted when a group of generals staged a *coup d'état* against the newly re-elected Republicans on 18 July 1936. Quite why Lorca was shot is a mystery: there was no explicit political charge against him. Gibson suggests that such was the macho ethic of the Granada Nationalists that he may have been killed for his homosexual reputation. Another possibility is that his drama, especially *Doña Rosita La Soltera*, had caused deep offence in Granada (this will be discussed later in this section). *Yerma*, as you will see, does not attack the Nationalists; but it struck at the roots of some of the principles they valued most.

*7.4*   It was not, however, just the conservatism of Spanish commercial theatre's themes, but the conservatism of its forms that Lorca revolutionized.

His experience with La Barraca also convinced him that, not only did existing audiences need to be re-educated, but new audiences sought outside the complacent middle classes:

> The theatre is one of the most expressive and useful vehicles for the edification of a country's people, and a barometer that marks the country's greatness or decline ... The theatre is a school of tears and laughter and an open tribunal where people can place outmoded or erroneous *mores* [manners and morals] on trial and explain through living examples the eternal standards of the human heart and feelings.
>
> (quoted in Anderson, 1984, p.28)

*7.5*  In some areas of the provinces where the company toured, anti-Republican interests tried to foment hostility. But for the most part, its reception was enthusiastic. Lorca was particularly encouraged by the reaction of audiences to the most stylized, least naturalistic aspects of his productions: 'for Lorca the restoration of poetry and moral seriousness to the stage was a conscious mission. It was in his practical efforts to achieve this and to restore the social vitality of the theatre that Lorca differed from all other contemporary dramatists in Spain' (Lyon, 1987, p.2).

*7.6*  'This whole idea of art for art's sake', he said, shortly before his death in 1936, 'is something that would be cruel if, fortunately, it weren't such an affectation ... At this dramatic moment in history the artist must weep and laugh with his people. He must lay aside his bouquet of lilies and plunge up to his waist into the mud to help those who are searching for lilies' (quoted in Anderson, 1984, p.33). He believed that theatre gave him direct contact with the masses, and that 'any theatre will only continue to be authentic as it moves along with the rhythms of its times, focusing the emotions, the suffering, the struggles, the dramas of those times...' (ibid., p.34). Yet, as you will see, *Yerma* is ostensibly about a world that time seems hardly to have touched. Just how it can be both so apparently removed from the main concerns of political debate and yet so ideologically subversive that its first production was a significant political event, is the main theme of this case-study.

*7.7*  In this study *language* is foregrounded as a key vehicle in the transmission of values, on the grounds that we acquire images, concepts and mental structures in the cradle, the home, at school and so on; and as adult language users, we actively reproduce what we have acquired. Language thus transmits the lived ideology. But so do beliefs and practices, and we shall also be examining aspects of male–female relationships among Lorca's characters, of the well-to-do peasant family, the church and superstition in a society that is very different from that of the UK.


## ACTIVITY

Your approach to the play *Yerma* should be to read it through first, paying particular attention not merely to the dialogue but equally to the playwright's detailed staging instructions, his use of lighting, mime, colour, song and human movement (Drama Anthology, pp.42–84).


## AUDIO-CASSETTE

Your next step is to listen carefully to the audio-cassette recording of three scenes drawn from the play (Audio-cassette 2 Side 2). Sadly our resources did not run to a television programme or a large cast (however, our small team included members of the Royal Shakespeare Company).

## DISCUSSION

Recording an English version of a Spanish play set in the pre-Civil War southern Spanish countryside brought us face to face with certain practical problems with ideological implications. Obviously there is no exactly equivalent British location or situation and it is not just that there is no precise political equivalent. The characters in *Yerma* could hardly be said to subscribe to any ideology in that sense. However, where in Britain is a community whose manner of living or 'lived' beliefs could be represented as an illuminating equivalent? Making the recording forced us to discern the 'lived' or 'customary' ideology because we had to adapt the play for a British audience.

The society of Lorca's play is much poorer materially; foods are basic, there are few soft furnishings – hence the hard sounds of floors and doors closing; religious concepts, like pilgrimage, are Catholic not Protestant; the domestic role of a married woman is obsessively concerned with child-bearing – and there is the problem of rural accents: in the recording, our central actor and actress use standard English pronunciation; we thereby run the risk of a class association, absent in the original Spanish. Alternatively, had we used a Barsetshire accent, we risked ridicule. A recent (1988) BBC drama broadcast set the play in the west of Ireland.

## ACTIVITY

Having explored the play, turn back to the beginning, look again at the title, subtitle, cast list and the detailed stage directions with which the play opens, and ask yourself what is particularly striking about Lorca's dramatic technique.

## DISCUSSION

I suspect that to those of us accustomed to documentary drama and soap operas, both strains of naturalistic drama, the overall purposes of which seem to include facsimile effects and the common-sense logic of our everyday lives, the opening of *Yerma* must come as a shock. By convention, the title is not translated. In fact Yerma is not a real name, but the feminine of the adjective *yermo* which means 'barren', and like the English word, it is an adjective applied to land and soil, carrying nuances of waste, wilderness, desert and absence of human habitation – in short, land or soil in need of water and the plough. There are further parallels with the English word that should be pursued: 'barren' is a native Anglo-Saxon word and its application to a woman now seems biblical; similarly, the Spanish *yermo* derives from the core vocabulary transmitted from Spain's early Vulgar Latin speaking inhabitants. It has therefore resonances of agricultural life, of peasant communities whose dependency upon the soil is absolute. The title links us to a sort of society now distanced by Spain's mini economic miracle of the 1960s.

The location of *Yerma* is accepted as the south of Spain, probably Granada, where the Arab past – surviving systems of irrigation and other evidence of their delight in water – is visible today. Of course, it may at first seem strange that the play's protagonist and eponymous heroine should bear the name of what is only gradually revealed to be an affliction; but a classical Greek parallel comes at once to mind: Oedipus, meaning 'club-foot'.

The play is further defined in its subtitle as a 'Tragic Poem in three acts and six scenes'. At first glance such a dramatic structure is conventional, invoking a long tradition of European verse drama. However, the Spanish word *cuadro*, translated as 'scene', strictly means 'picture'. The dramatic structure contains, then, a visual imperative: we must look as well as listen. Furthermore, the stage directions of the first scene, in a manner typical of Lorca's craftsmanship, are very detailed: there is mime to convey the atmosphere of a dream, the chiming of a clock, a children's lullaby sung off-stage, and stage lighting manipulated to achieve the light of a cheerful spring morning. Lorca was an able musician and draughtsman. In the 1920s he had collaborated with the Surrealist painter Salvador Dalí, and had incorporated surrealist techniques in his poetry, notably in the *Gipsy Ballads.* Lorca was using a commercial theatre, but had the confidence to challenge a public that might have expected conventional naturalistic drama. The setting of the opening scene forced the involvement of the audience's dominant senses and employed a sort of staged surrealism in order to draw attention to the protagonist, Yerma's, unconscious mind during sleep. Lorca, like others working through the aesthetic of Surrealism, broadly took for granted the structure of mind that we associate with Freud.

The cast list may well make us pause too. Most have no names but are defined by their sex or their work. Your translation keeps the original organization of the cast list: the females precede the males, a significant detail overlooked in the recent (1986) National Theatre production. Only the nuclear family consisting of Juan and Yerma and three outsiders, Dolores, María and Víctor, are named. I infer that a Spaniard, reverting to the cast list after reading the play, would also notice that an old woman (in the Spanish, she is pagan, not Christian), the cheerful old woman of Act I, scene ii, reappears at the fertility pilgrimage in the final scene. Spain was reputedly a deeply Catholic society; the late General Franco called the Nationalist uprising, in 1936, a crusade. Lorca however has suppressed the rites and representatives of the Catholic Church; in the other two plays of what is commonly called Lorca's 'rural trilogy', *Blood Wedding* and *The House of Bernarda Alba*, no members of the church appear either, and church-related activities seem to be decorative and secondary to more elemental human forces. The cast list draws our attention to social roles and contains implicit challenges to conventional views of the importance of the Church.

## Home

*ACTIVITY*

Now please read again the first scene of the play and, as you do so, try to articulate for yourself some of the essential features of young married womanhood, the nature of the emerging tension between Yerma and Juan, and relevant aspects of the dramatist's skill.

*DISCUSSION*

I think we would all agree that in the society portrayed in the play, a young married woman's first concern is to bear children; she achieves social identity and fulfilment through motherhood. The young wife is housebound in a strictly monogamous relationship. In *Blood Wedding* the Bridegroom's Mother epitomizes a wife's role in society with the words:

a husband, children and a wall two yards thick for everything else

(I.iii)

On hearing the news of María's pregnancy so soon after marrying, Yerma shares her joy and offers advice and help.

Perhaps an initial appraisal of the nature of the tension between Yerma and Juan is that she longs to be a mother and he appears fretful of her advances and affection, states explicitly that the farm is doing well, and it is a good thing that there are no children to run away with the money. In fact the play is partly an exploration of the relationship between Yerma and Juan over several years and for this reason we must be prepared subsequently to qualify this appraisal. Their marriage is an arranged marriage between better-off peasantry as in *Blood Wedding*, the basis of which is economic alliance. In the subsequent scene (I. ii), Yerma confesses to the old woman:

> my son will fulfil my dreams. It's for his sake that I gave myself to my husband, and I go on giving myself in the hope my child will come, but never, never, for pleasure.

Only some years before, at fourteen, when Víctor the shepherd had helped her cross a ditch, could she recall experiencing sexual arousal. And Yerma hopes for a son, not a daughter, an instance of social conditioning that you could reflect on further. Maternity is not enough.

Those aspects of the dramatist's skill that have especially struck me in this opening scene, include a choice of language that evokes a rural community dependent on staples like sheep, wheat and olives, and on soil and rain; there are concepts that recur, linking and polarizing: water in various forms, growth, as against dryness and withering decay. Human sexuality and childbearing are part of this natural world. Lorca exercises great artistic freedom, moving easily between mime, nursery song, domestic dialogue and more highly charged prose, an aesthetic blend that catches and holds unconscious states, psychic and emotional conditions. There is the subtle hinting of a sub-text: the shepherd of the mime is perhaps Víctor the shepherd, whose air Yerma seeks to breathe. And there is a larger, universalizing motif, when, for example, Yerma identifies herself with all women who do not have children saying, in the Spanish, that their blood turns to poison; in the next scene, she tells the Old Woman that she is filling up with hatred. Yerma's predicament is enlarged to embrace womankind and convey foreboding and inevitability.

## Village laundering

### ACTIVITY

I ask you now to read again the first scene of Act II together with the illuminating translator's notes on Spanish country laundering, and as you do so, to reflect upon the dramatic purpose or importance of the scene.

### DISCUSSION

Lorca has invoked a very old tradition of drama and opera (and surely the singing gives the scene an operatic quality): the chorus that comments upon the heroine places her within the wider society and advances the action. Juan has brought his two spinster sisters to live with them because Yerma cannot 'stay put in her own house', he is concerned for his reputation and his sisters caricature certain transmitted values and social practices. They join the washerwomen but utter no dialogue.

Yerma's household is an object of community fascination and gossip, a gaol or hell, and a sort of emotional bomb. The chorus is not a consistent whole, the first washerwoman being well-meaning and more hesitant to judge; but the overall impression conveyed is of a blend of cruelty, cynicism and contempt for a childless woman tangled in a marriage from which no escape is possible. The mixture of song and stychomythic repartee (i.e. answering single lines of verse dialogue, a Senecan technique) that concludes the scene aesthetically mirrors erotic love-making and female fertility, thus reinforcing this rural society's predominant concern with procreation.

There are aspects of the language that continue and develop matters discussed in relation to the first scene of the play. The chorus does not name Yerma, Juan or his sisters – they are referred to in the terminology of marital status: the husband, the spinsters, 'she'. 'She' is further defined in terms that question her conformity to sexual norms: the word in Spanish is *machorras*, translated for you as 'these barren women', but this word, which could well be a coinage of Lorca's, seems to be a feminized pejorative of the word *macho*, male. There are, then, nuances of sexual inadequacy and 'unfeminine' aggression. The Fourth Woman later says: 'It's her fault, she's got a tongue like a flint', and in Act II, scene ii Yerma tells María 'when I walk through the yard in the dark my footsteps sound like a man's'. In our discussion of the opening scene, we noted Lorca's concern for total staging. This is equally in evidence in the chorus scene: your translation says that Yerma's two sisters-in-law come on dressed in black, but the Spanish reads 'dressed in mourning', and the references to death surely contrast sharply with the scene's foregrounding of eroticism, fertility and procreation. Indeed, immediately after the sisters-in-law have entered, we learn that the shepherds have united their flocks and are leaving. The Fourth Woman remarks:

> I love the smell of sheep
> … the smell of what's mine. Just as I
> love the smell of the red mud that comes down
> with the river in wintertime.

The fecund smell of greasy sheep is a sexual reference surely carried further by the references to red mud and water. The sea of wool and the green cornstalks of wheat carry on the theme of nature's abundance. Only one flock is missing, Víctor's. Shortly after, the First Woman cries out: 'Have pity on the barren wife', but the Spanish actually reads: 'Alas for the dry married woman', a phrase she repeats towards the end. In the opening of the next scene (II.ii), we learn that Yerma has gone out to the fountain, she tells Juan she wants to drink water and tells María, 'you've no idea of what it is to thirst'.

This cry for water must be set against the Fourth Woman's joyful description of the sheep – 'a sea of wool' (literally 'a flooding'). She then employs a verb normally used only of a rushing river, when the head of water brings down sand and gravel – in your translation: 'Sweeping everything along on its tide.'

This deluge of life-giving energy must be set against Juan's words to Yerma at the opening of the next scene:

> Don't you know what sort of man I am?
> Sheep in the fold, and women in the house.

Lorca's creative energy has bound together recurring images and motifs that in turn identify patterns of values. There is a satisfying aesthetic tightness in structure, yet the play is not 'closed off'. To pick up the cruel discussion of the chorus, does blame for the childlessness reside with Yerma or Juan? Or neither?

# Pilgrimage

## *ACTIVITY*

I now move on to the final scene of the play (III.ii) and ask you to read it afresh, bearing in mind the discussion so far.

Consider the range of linguistic dictions deployed, the evidence of author as director, how this scene brings to a climax and resolves tensions at the heart of the play; and what kinds of reflections an audience might carry with it from the theatre, reflections for example upon the condition of married women, male dominance and the structures of beliefs and practices exposed.

## *DISCUSSION*

The scene depicts a pilgrimage to a local religious shrine, but the occasion has pagan associations which are intended to promote fertility, in a way that entirely obliterates conventional religious observance. The song before the curtain rises is sung by a male voice and addresses a female pilgrim, a married woman, whom the singer will strip in the darkness when the clock strikes twelve. The earthy, pagan Old Woman – the cheerful Old Woman of Act I – reveals the nature of the cure for fertility when she comments upon the increasing number of unaccompanied males ('single' in the text) who turn up. María speaks of a 'river of men' – notice again the water image.

The final scene provides, in rapid sequence, irreligious bawdry, down-to-earth comic prose, then a series of prayers offered to the Lord, which Yerma joins in. The prayers are shaped as poetry of basically eight syllables in Spanish metrics, and the Male and Female masks continue the poetic form, but substituting erotic lyric material for religious invocation. It is, I suggest, very important to try to capture the shocking effect of such a juxtaposition and rapid sequence of linguistic codes, and of clashing inherent norms and values, especially those of conventional morality, underwritten by the Church, and of a sexual freedom presented as a vital and pagan alternative. You will appreciate why the right-wing press reacted to the first performance by denouncing the play as blasphemous.

I expect you registered Lorca's continuing use of images of water and dryness. Your translation, an effective acting text, falls back on the single word 'barren' where the Spanish has *seca* – dry (married woman) and *marchita* – faded, an adjective usually used of flowers and here applied to flesh and the womb. You may have noticed the importance of the language of flowers, which to an English reader recalls Renaissance literature, a pre-industrial society.

Lorca has given very detailed stage directions governing the entrance of the Male and Female masks and it is only sensible to ponder authorial intentions: Lorca wants the masks to be modelled from Spanish folk tradition, not high art and not caricature; he wants to convey a beauty and an association with the soil. During their erotic exchange guitars strike up and, I infer, body language, rhythm, posture and the use of space have some similarity to the flamenco work most of us have seen. The stage audience join in with their cries and clapping of encouragement. It is tempting to regard this piece of drama within a drama as a sort of inversion or parody of a religious ceremony too, and expressive of a freedom beyond society's conventions.

At this point, Yerma re-enters, dejected, and the Old Woman invites her to come and live with her son. Yerma can no more accept than she could join the dance. Notice her response:

I'm like a parched field. Big enough to hold a thousand teams of
oxen ploughing and you're offering me a tiny glass of stagnant
water! My pain is more than flesh deep.

Yerma is bound by family honour and must reject the opportunity of
adultery. Her subsequent frenzied murder of her husband ends all hope of
motherhood, hence her final words.

## ACTIVITY

We come now to a wider reflection. I ask you to look back to the
introduction, and to assess whether a critical approach that addresses certain
beliefs, practices and social structures in a southern Spanish peasant society,
and foregrounds language in the transmission of values, illuminates the play
and offers some explanation of its impact on the audience.

## DISCUSSION

My own response is that such an approach helps us to articulate aspects of
the rural world of *Yerma* that may in turn bring to our own consciousness,
and challenge, some of our own rooted assumptions, beliefs and practices,
though our society may be quite different.

Yerma is a young married woman in a society in which motherhood is the
key female role and which, historically, has been characterized by enormous
stress on breeding. She has internalized – or in Althusser's term interpellated
– beliefs, values and attitudes about the married woman, motherhood and
childbearing. Remember her words:

> Some girls I know trembled and wept before going to bed with their
> husbands for the first time. Did I weep the first time I slept with
> you? Didn't I sing as I turned back the linen sheets? And didn't I
> say: 'What a glorious smell of apples these bedclothes have!'
>
> (I.i)

and:

> My husband is different. My father chose him for me and I accepted.
> Joyfully. That's the absolute truth. Because from the very first day we
> got engaged I thought about … having children … And I looked at
> my reflection in his eyes. But I saw myself very tiny and submissive,
> as if I were looking at my own daughter.
>
> (I.ii)

Yerma's marriage was arranged: in her own words she joyfully accepted this.
Yerma has submitted to the point of treating the social demands made on her
as common sense and seeking confirmation, from her husband and from the
Old Woman, of the rightness of her beliefs. She seeks, literally, to reproduce
the social structure of which she is victim. Yerma, the female protagonist, is
tragically interesting from our ideological viewpoint because she is suffering
at the point where the individual and society engage: she wants children, she
and her husband do not have them; and the same society that induced the
drive for motherhood equally insists upon monogamy and 'honour', or
marital fidelity as we may be more inclined to say. Yerma is the victim of a
subtle and tragic oppression, but in a larger sense she portrays how people
may be coerced into wishing to reproduce the causes of their oppression.

There is an important balancing consideration. Much contemporary feminist
writing stresses a woman's right to control her own body, often in the context

of the right to restrict her fertility or indeed not to have any children at all. However, part of the cultural difficulty with Act III, scene ii of *Yerma* is that an English and especially Protestant audience does not immediately perceive that in parts of Spain festive pilgrimages were (and sometimes still are) regarded as opportunities for childless married women to make compensatory arrangements. Innocents' Day (28 December) also had this association. The play is a legitimate reminder that a woman's right to determine the destiny of her own body may indeed take the form of a demand to seek fulfilment in fertility.

The particular ideological focus adopted here may be additionally illuminating if applied in parallel to other texts in this block. Fugard, Kani and Ntshona's *The Island* reworks the Antigone myth, adapting the story in order to polarize conflict between individual and state, much as Lorca polarizes wife and husband, woman and society. Meursault in Camus's *The Outsider* is conspicuous because, within the same focus, he appears to have acquired no affective bonds or clear beliefs – he is a sort of ideological void. Perhaps in practice there is no such person as an ideologically free or untainted individual and the literary experiment of attempting to imagine such a person leads us into medical conjecture. If a person like Meursault really lived, perhaps he would be emotionally, mentally and socially sick.

## First night

### ACTIVITY

How does (or should) a writer react to an extreme political situation? You have already considered the question in relation to some of the English writers of the thirties in Block 3. To extend the debate, look now at the extract from Sartre's *What is Literature?* in the Reader (pp.202–6). In this chapter, Sartre considers the moral dilemmas that faced artists in the thirties during the rise of Fascism, the agonizing choices faced by the French writing during the occupation, and the (then current) post-war situation. You need only read the first part ('We've started feeling this gap … a literature of a historical character', pp.202–3), though of course the whole extract is relevant to the theme of the block.

Sartre vividly describes how a new consciousness of their place in future history overcame the artists of his circle. Although you have been supplied with only the sketchiest of information, how far do you think his observations might be relevant to Lorca?

### DISCUSSION

When Sartre says 'we had no choice but to produce a literature of a historical character' he clearly doesn't mean costume drama, but a literature responsive to historical circumstances. Lorca's play may at first glance seem ahistorical, even 'timeless', but for him too, surely, 'the holiday was over'. He could not write the trite fashionable plays that 'idle souls wanted', but turned instead to those occupied without respite with a single concern – his country's peasants. This may help you to understand how *Yerma* was received at its first performance.

Carlos Morla Lynch, who at that time was Chilean ambassador in Madrid, recorded the atmosphere surrounding the opening night of *Yerma* in his diary entry for 29 December 1934, as follows:

Today, everything has revolved around the first performance of *Yerma*. Tickets have sold out and resale prices are soaring ... Federico has been on edge all day. There are rumours that a hostile demonstration is being organized which could make the play a disaster; I think on the contrary, it might even add to its success. Of course, there are people who are envious and resentful of the brilliant career of a young man whose talent has overcome all obstacles in his path. Besides, Federico has publicly declared himself as belonging to 'the party of the poor', that is, of the unfortunate, a statement which has been wilfully misconstrued by some as political ... Another source of anxiety is that Margarita Xirgu[1] who will play the part of Yerma, has put the house she owns in Catalonia at the disposal of Señor Azaña[2], who had just been released after his arrest. It is a kind gesture, beyond reproach. We all have the right to offer our hospitality to whomsoever we wish and think fit, especially in times of trouble ... In the street opposite the Teatro Español there is tremendous activity and a feeling that something sensational is about to happen. Streams of taxis and private cars stop briefly in front of the main entrance and then pull away. Inside the theatre, as in the case of *Bodas de sangre* [Blood Wedding], there is a full house. Again, as last year, all the intelligentsia are present, plus the usual few aristocratic ladies of independent mind (some six or seven at most), and almost all the diplomatic community. Greetings; handshakes; friendly, open smiles. Then the lights go out: night and silence. The curtain goes up...

(quoted in MacPherson and Minett, 1987, pp.27–8)

Lynch's diary entry is a fascinating piece of evidence, telling us as much about Lynch himself as about the first performance of *Yerma* and its public reception. He was of part-Irish ancestry, a close friend of Lorca, who moved in the cultural circle that embraced the Madrid avant-garde. Yet his own diplomatic and cultural prejudices are evident. He may – as many Latin Americans have done – affect contempt for European aristocracy, especially its female portion, but he betrays anxiety that an actress should have offered hospitality to a fallen and sick Republican politician and that *Yerma* should have been 'wilfully misconstrued by some as political'. He wishes to separate art and politics as, for example, late Victorian aesthetes tried to do. Lynch betrays the understandable timidity of his diplomatic status and middle-class origins.

In fact, the first performance of *Yerma* was an event of international significance (almost all the Madrid diplomatic community was present). Artistic works may be subversive by intent or by accident. *Yerma* was artistically subversive because in form and subject-matter it challenged theatre-going preference for Spanish operetta (*zarzuela*) and 'well made' plays full of bourgeois conventions. However *Yerma* inevitably became caught in the politically charged atmosphere of Spain: the government was weak and had experienced collapse in September 1934. Franco had brutally crushed a revolt of miners in Asturias (autumn 1934), strikes were widespread and endemic, Catalans staged an uprising – also suppressed – Basques sought local autonomy and anarchism remained strong in Aragón. Of particular significance to the public performance of *Yerma* was rising unemployment and employer intransigence leading to an agricultural labourers' strike, which also collapsed quickly. In 1934 Spain was in the process of political polarization, at the one extreme the military, Fascism and elements in Catholicism, at the other, Socialism, becoming more radical and revolutionary, in loose coalition with more moderate Republican reformers, anarchists, separatists and communists. *Yerma's* first performance therefore acquired a sensational quality, testing the elasticity or fragility of Spanish society. In an atmosphere

[1]Margarita Xirgu was a Catalán actress and impresario of progressive views. Lorca had written *Yerma* expressely with her in mind for the leading role.

[2]Manuel Azaña, formerly head of the Republican Government, had been arrested in October 1934, allegedly for incitement to revolution in Catalonia.

of social and political polarization and approaching civil war, it seemed to many to subvert traditional values – which many Spaniards idealized and located in rural society.

As a dramatist, Lorca was associated with the radical avant-garde that wished to break the conventions of commercial theatre. He had taken plays to country towns and villages. The second Republican Government had funded this work. In his poetry Lorca had expressed strong anti-clerical feeling and support for underprivileged groups, like the blacks in the USA and gypsies in Spain. In press announcements, as well as his theatre, Lorca attacked middle-class smugness. Small wonder that the right-wing press attacked the play. Ian Gibson has observed:

> When [Lorca's] rural tragedy *Yerma* was staged ... in Madrid, the reactionary press refused without exception to acknowledge the author's talent and claimed that his work was immoral, anti-Catholic, irrelevant to Spain's problems and lacking in verisimilitude.
>
> (Gibson, 1983, p.34)

Almost one year later, 12 December 1935, his next full, new play *Doña Rosita La Soltera o El Lenguaje De Las Flores* ('Miss Rosie the spinster or the language of flowers') exposed the Granada middle classes. It was first performed in Barcelona.

Nonetheless, Lorca was not committed to a political ideology in the conventional sense. Like a number of Spanish intellectuals, he had welcomed the Second Republic in 1931 and closely identified with its aspirations; he joined protests against international Fascism – for instance by cancelling a cultural tour to Italy – in reaction to Mussolini's invasion of Abyssinia in 1935; he publicly supported the Popular Front in 1936 and liberal causes abroad, especially in Latin America. Yet his political statements, such as they were, convey more a general concern for justice, democracy, social peace and harmony. One summer's afternoon in 1935, he was challenged to define himself politically and said:

> I am an anarchist, libertarian communist, pagan Catholic, traditionalist and monarchist supporter of Don Duarte of Portugal.
>
> (quoted in McDermott, 1988, note on p.78)

He spoke in fun but with more than a grain of truth. He was an artist and entertainer as well as a revolutionary and *enfant terrible* of the theatre. Indeed, he criticized his contemporary, the poet Alberti, who had returned from Russia as a communist, remarking:

> ...he no longer writes poetry, although he believes he does, but bad magazine literature ... The artist and especially the poet, is always an anarchist in the best sense of the word...
>
> (quoted in McDermott, 1988, p.75; this extract translated by Keith Whitlock)

This statement anticipates Theodor Adorno's discussion of commitment in the final section of this block.

# 8    Ideology and 'The Island'

*8.1*    The aim of this section is twofold: firstly, to introduce you to the study of *The Island*, a play 'devised by Athol Fugard, John Kani and Winston Ntshona', as the title-page states; secondly, to use your study of the play to develop further your ideas about the relevance and application of the term 'ideology' to literary or dramatic texts. Since no study can be ideology-free, I will address these two aims simultaneously. Broadly, my argument will be that, while the play appears to be explicitly 'ideological' in the simple sense of opposing the apartheid system, it may also be understood to engage with 'ideology' on a deeper, sometimes contradictory level, when approached for example from the perspective suggested by Theodor Adorno, who raises the question of the nature and validity of modern literature, and specifically drama (his main example is Brecht), in 'so-called extreme situations' (Reader, p.96). Adorno had in mind the literature which came into being in response to the atrocities of the Second World War , and which attempted to engage with those events ; but the South African situation, while at last transforming itself, has long sustained comparable realms of extremity for the many individuals caught up in the webs of apartheid. I will be looking especially at the production of the play, in the Marxist sense explained by Terry Eagleton in the reading you studied in Section 1; and I will be considering its 'gaps' and 'silences' in the Machereyan sense (see Reader, pp.215–22).

*8.2*    The relevance and applicability of the term 'ideology' in the simple sense should be immediately apparent from the subject and setting of *The Island*. If you have not already read or looked at the play, you could try just opening the first two or three pages of the text. As you can see, it is about two black political prisoners who themselves put on a play in the notorious maximum security gaol on Robben Island, South Africa. I expect you to find that, from the moment you begin, you will be aware of being transported to a milieu and mode of thinking and speaking – to a reality – unlike any you have met so far on the course. This experience is central to how the play engages with ideology in the more profound sense. It is also part of the point of choosing a text which comes from outside the European, or Anglo-American, centres of power.

*8.3*    We will be discussing this point further in Block 6, in which the major texts are all from 'abroad' in this sense, and may be said to represent the phenomenal development of 'literatures in English' as opposed to 'English literature'. Another point to bear in mind is the fact that this text is therefore also not part of the recognized 'canon' of English literature; although, of course, that is not an absolutely hard-and-fast or static thing and *The Island* may be in the process of becoming 'canonized'.

*8.4*    Thus, for example, although it was first performed on the 2 July 1973 in the then obscure venue of 'The Space' in Cape Town, *The Island* reappeared within six months (on 12 December) as the second of three so-called 'Statements', plays by Fugard, Kani and Ntshona in what was billed as a South African season at the Royal Court theatre in London – a season which, within a year, had achieved world-wide renown for its co-creators and performers, including appearances in New York and elsewhere on stage and in the media. It was followed by publication of all the texts of the play in the Oxford University Press (1974) version we are using here. By choosing it as a set text, we are contributing to this process of 'canonization' – which, it could be argued, diffuses somewhat its overt ideological impact, by incorporating it into the institution of the literary classic.

## The main issue

*8.5* The achievement and international reputation of the white South African playwright Athol Fugard is now certain. The same cannot be said of John Kani and Winston Ntshona, for reasons that will become obvious, although Kani is now Associate Director of the prestigious multi-racial Market Theatre (Johannesburg) and a well-known actor outside his country. Ten years after the two black South Africans shared a Tony award for their performances in *The Island* on Broadway, these extraordinarily talented men were described in the local press as follows: 'Mr Kani has done three plays in three years, Mr Ntshona has done none. He runs his grocery store in New Brighton' (a segregated black 'township' on the outskirts of Port Elizabeth, South Africa). The occasion of this report was a revival of the play with its original cast at the Baxter Theatre in Cape Town, in a production accompanied by the following programme note, which was quoted in Cape Town's *Weekend Argus* on 2 November, 1985:

> We, John Kani and Winston Ntshona, declare every single performance of this play, *The Island*, as an endorsement of the local and international call for the immediate release of Mr Nelson Mandela and all political prisoners and detainees. We earnestly hope that this call will receive the support of all well-meaning South Africans.

Perhaps nothing could more clearly indicate how the two co-creators later viewed their performances in this play, and, further, how they 'earnestly' hoped that their audiences would too: as the 'endorsement' of a specific political action.

*8.6* As you might expect, others viewed (and still view) it differently. The simplest response was provoked by the first 'season' of all three 'Statements' plays; the *Eastern Province Herald* reported on 5 February 1974:

> Weekend Press reports said the South African Embassy had received complaints from people alleging that Fugard's season of plays at the Royal Court Theatre in Chelsea contained propaganda aimed at discrediting the South African Embassy in London, the Government, and White South Africans in general.

Neither the South African Embassy, the Government, nor 'White South Africans in general' are mentioned anywhere in the play – neither, of course, is Mandela's name, which was still anathema at the time. If the 'international call' for his release had become, by the time of the Kani/Ntshona revival, something they could echo (one result of the superficial easing of apartheid during the interim), the first production of the play was undoubtedly interpreted locally and in London by sympathizers of the regime as an attack upon the explicit ideology of apartheid and its supporters.

*8.7* Does this mean simply that your response to the play depends upon whether you support apartheid or are opposed to it? Yes. But things aren't quite so simple. If they were, then you might want to dismiss the play as polemic or propaganda – although propaganda does have its place. But more subtle responses were also evident, reflecting an awareness that the nature of the play somehow generalized the specifically South African experience. 'Fugard and his colleagues', observed one critic of the Royal Court season, 'almost alone among contemporary South African writers, are able to universalize experience' (Niven, 1975). This response was taken a step further by the author of a subsequent critical study: 'The problems ... are ultimately metaphysical', was how this critic summed up the same group of plays (Vandenbroucke, 1985, p.147). The implication is clear: the play transcends, even if it also includes, the category of propaganda. Or, we may say, these critics have discerned in it an element of autonomy, an autonomy essential to any definition of great art.

8.8   Fugard's own position has varied, from stating baldly that 'I am not using the stage as a political platform' (*Eastern Province Herald*, 5 February 1974) to a more ambivalent insistence that 'writing is a form of action' if a 'long-term investment' (Benson, 1983, p.223). The position I took in my own introductory study, *Athol Fugard* (1984), was that *The Island* 'suggests that men may survive the most intolerable conditions if they are able to discover and articulate a meaning for their suffering'; and that while the play may appear to have 'universal implications' for overseas audiences, for South Africans its message was 'more direct, an expression of solidarity with their banned and imprisoned leaders' (pp.76, 90). Broadly speaking, this remains my view: but it needs some development, which I will try to provide here.

8.9   As I see it, the main issue is how, in the light of what I've just told you about the play, we, as students of it at this distance in time and place from its production(s), should understand and respond to it. As in some sense a 'timeless', or even 'metaphysical' work of art? Or does your experience of the play perhaps suggest that these are meaningless extremes? Might it rather depend upon your own position in relation to that experience, an experience mediated to you by this course? Might it also, then, depend upon how you define(d) your beliefs, your own ideology, in response? And what do we make of the fact that this noticeably modern play draws upon one of the most ancient, 'classical' dramas of Western culture, Sophocles' *Antigone*? You should find yourself progressing towards some answers to these questions as you work through this section of the block.

## What kind of play?

### ACTIVITY

Let's begin by turning directly to the play-text itself. *The Island* is a short work, and I would like you now to read it straight through (Drama Anthology pp.240–71). You can ignore any words and phrases or allusions you don't understand, but remember that, as with all drama read 'on the page', you should pay attention to *stage directions*, and at least start to imagine what it is you would be seeing on stage. What is your first impression?

### DISCUSSION

I can't tell you what your first impression will be, of course. But I can report that most, if not all, of the audiences before whom the play has been performed have found it a shattering experience. Remarks such as 'shocking', 'terrible', 'appalling' are common, and not only from those who assume they agree with its 'message'. So, too, are words such as 'moving', and 'uplifting' – in the sense, perhaps, of 'I've been to hell and back, and it's good to be back'; but perhaps also, 'I feel I know something of what human beings can stand, and survive'. At any rate, it's undeniably powerful, isn't it? And, as these comments might suggest, it provokes more than simply one feeling, although shock might well be the first and most lasting, *in the theatre*.

But we are not in the theatre; although we have to imagine what our play is like there, since, like all plays, this has been created for (and, as we shall see, in a sense *by*) performance. Having the written text before us means that we are offered a certain distance, and time, to consider the emotions first aroused by it. But I don't think any consideration should lose our first response. What we can do is try to analyse that response, in order to understand better how it was produced, and to what ends. This enables us, among other things, to pursue the ideological potential of the play, which involves that of our own position at the same time.

Because, if we are shocked, that means our expectations have been affected; and where did those expectations come from? From our previous experience which, obviously, includes, and arguably has been shaped by, our basic assumptions about the world we live in – in other words, by ideology, in the profound sense. We all, often quite unconsciously, adopt an approach to what we see or read which depends upon what we think we are seeing or reading *for*. In relation to this play, our response may depend upon our expectations in the more limited sense of ideology – in that we arrive at it already holding some view about the South African situation with which it deals so openly and powerfully, and which is then confirmed or overturned by it. Or – and this I want to explore later – our response may also depend upon less obvious, more complex and perhaps contradictory views.

To return to the play in more detail: the basic action reflects a relatively simple and strong dramatic rhythm, revolving around the shifting relationship between the two men as they part and come together again and again. But how, precisely, does this action begin?

## ACTIVITY

Please re-read the opening, unusually lengthy, stage directions.

What impact might this opening have? What function does it serve? And, arising from your answers to these questions, what kind of play would you say we have here – traditional/naturalistic/modern/symbolic or other?

## DISCUSSION

The opening mime invariably creates something of a shock in itself, anticipating as well as preparing us for what's to come. A memorable image of horror, of hell, is conveyed by the siren, harsh lights and whistle-commands from the dark which control these two humiliated creatures, whose shaven heads and schoolboy shorts reinforce their pathetic dependency. Their futile labour is strongly reminiscent of those endless tasks which occupy the damned in the familiar, traditional, Judaeo-Christian conception of hell. The fact that the play concludes with the same image reinforces this sense of endless suffering, barely interrupted by what has happened in between.

Does this circularity perhaps *undermine* the protest implied by putting on the play-within-the-play in the prison? We'll come back to this point. But what the question immediately suggests is that there is an ideological dimension to the *form* of the work – which is, I trust you'll agree, 'modern', or, if you prefer, 'Modernist', in the same way that, say, *Endgame* is: exemplifying an aesthetic of non-naturalistic discourse, in which the non-verbal, repetitive, uncluttered (i.e. by costume, props or sets) dramatic 'event' is dominant; in which the sub-textual, symbolic gesture communicates as much if not more than overt speech; and in which a characteristically self-conscious, self-referential element is central. The play, as you will quickly have realized, is as much *about* drama – and the point or function of drama – as it is about anything. Further, like certain other 'modernist' works – from *The Waste Land*, to *Madmen and Specialists*, to 'Crow' – *The Island* draws on myth, specifically the bloody feuds of classical Greek myth embodied in the work of Sophocles, and, like them, it does so in order to find a meaning for the intolerable, the incomprehensible.

But, you may well object, unlike those other works, *The Island* has a palpable design upon us, and it deals with a real place, with known suffering, enacted, yes, but enacted by people who, as black South Africans, are drawing upon their actual experience. This is deeply embedded in the texture of the dialogue which, as you cannot avoid noticing, is determinedly 'local' – hence the need, for an overseas audience such as ourselves, of the glossary we have provided, to explain the meaning of terms such as 'Hodoshe', 'punkies' and so on; phrases such as 'Hell, ons was gemoer vandag' (Afrikaans, literally: 'we were fucked today') or 'Nyana we Sizwe' (Xhosa: 'Son of the Land'); and places such as 'St George's Strand' and 'New Brighton'. Does this imply a 'naturalistic' tendency after all? An attempt to reflect the everyday details of the lives of those characters the play is about? And if so, does it then carry the associated ideological implications too: that here we have a 'reflection' of certain realities, appalling, but also a 'slice of life', inexorably given?

Up to a point, perhaps yes. But we surely cannot forget who the actors were – or should I say are? The answer depends upon the performance, the historical event, we are talking about.

## ACTIVITY

Are we considering the first, or one of the originating productions, with the co-creators Kani and Ntshona? Or one of their own later versions, after the writing down of the text? Or later productions, by other performers, in South Africa, or abroad? Are we talking about the same play in all these cases? Pause and think about your answer to the last question.

## DISCUSSION

Yes – and no, I would say. What these questions highlight is the sense in which the text in hand, or the 'literary' text, is incomplete. It is, perhaps, best considered as a kind of record or document, rather than some essential 'play-in-itself'. But it is, then, a document with holes that yawn open every time we are brought to realize that John and Winston are two real people whose personal histories include the people and places the actors refer to in their roles as 'John' and 'Winston' – 'My little Monde', 'Georgie', 'Mulligan', 'St Stephen's Hall', 'Sky's place', and so on. The text we have is not, and cannot be 'complete'. One way of discovering a more 'complete' idea of it would be to find out about its conditions of production, which is what I would like to turn to next.

## Authorship and ideology

8.10  I'm using 'production' here not just in the familiar theatrical sense, but in the sense of the play's origins, its 'authorship', as well as the conditions of its first performance. Ideally, we could then go on to consider its 'consumption' or reception; and, finally, its 'status' or value. But there isn't the room to do more than touch on these dimensions of it. These terms come from an approach with which you may be familiar (especially if you studied A102). It is an approach resting on two assumptions implicit in the European-Marxist tradition of cultural criticism exemplified for our purposes by Adorno and Macherey: firstly, that the meaning and value of a text is itself a cultural construct, not simply given, or always the same; and secondly, that in responding to and interpreting artworks, we need to look beyond the explicit, or even implicit political content, towards a particular use of aesthetic conventions, and the work's position in relation to other, contemporaneous cultural practices. In this way, we can expose those limitations, those 'silences' (as Macherey calls them), which reveal the ideology lying behind the work and which speak through it; also, perhaps, those strengths which might make it a continuing provocation.

*8.11* How did the 'gaps' I've mentioned come about, then? And what do they tell us? The answers are implicit in that phrase you may already have puzzled about: the claim on the title-page that this play was 'devised by Athol Fugard, John Kani and Winston Ntshona'. The triple authorship obscures at the same time as it alerts us to a particular, indeed unique conjunction of personal, social and historical factors which produced this text, and which may be said to have 'inscribed' its ideologies.

*8.12* It seems obvious to begin, as the title-page does, with the first name. Who is Athol Fugard, where does he come from, what is his position? Before providing the answers, it is worth pointing out that this already implies a predominant, even determining, role for the white co-creator. Remember this as you read what follows.

*8.13* Athol Fugard has long been the best-known and most important playwright to emerge from South Africa. His plays (nineteen at present, including co-productions) have usually been performed first in his own country under his direction and with himself in a leading role. Like a writer he strongly admires, Albert Camus, Fugard belongs by birth and upbringing to the underprivileged sector of the dominant minority of his country: in Camus's case, this minority was the source of the most virulent anti-Arab feelings in pre-independence Algeria; in Fugard's case, of the most persistent anti-black feelings in South Africa. Both found themselves, as artists, turning against their own group's apparent interests. Despite a small-town, Afrikaans background, Fugard was brought up and educated in an English-speaking environment, and chose to write in English or, more accurately, in a South African idiom reflecting both the uncertainty and the potential of his culture by mingling English, Afrikaans and African (specifically, Xhosa) speech.

*8.14* What is meant by 'his culture'? In talking about South Africa, one is talking about a fragmented, ex-colonial culture, in which the potential for unity and integration among its variety of peoples has not only been resisted for centuries by the dominant white minority, but which has also been undermined by an explicit ideology emphasizing and exploiting historical divisions in terms of racial difference. This is the ideology of apartheid, of course; a collection of racist beliefs not in themselves unique, but whose brutally systematic application to a whole society certainly is. How do artists, writers, dramatists connect with this 'culture'? That depends upon their background, race and 'politics'.

*8.15* Fugard's 'politics' are 'liberal'; or, to be more precise (the word means different things in different cultures and countries), 'white liberal'. And, as his 'white liberal' compatriot, the writer Nadine Gordimer, has remarked:

> there is no country in the western world where the daily enactment of the law reflects politics as intimately and as blatantly as in South Africa. There is no country in the western world where the creative imagination, whatever it seizes upon, finds the focus of even the most private event set in the overall social determination of racial laws.

As she went on to suggest, white South Africans like herself 'are born twice', the second time when they emerge from the racism that was 'as "natural" to them as the walls of home and school' (Heywood, 1976, pp. 100, 110). In other words, into an ideological awareness, which goes beyond simply recognizing the immorality of apartheid, but which has to do with a change in *consciousness*, with a subversion of what formerly seemed 'given' or 'natural'. The play that made Fugard's name, *The Blood Knot* (1961), for example, opens with an extended mime in which the most familiar 'natural', relationship in South Africa is subverted: a 'white' man behaves like a housekeeper, a domestic servant, to a 'black' – it turns out that they are two 'coloured' or mixed-race brothers, tormented by their relationship in a racist society. It seems unlikely to be a coincidence that *The Island* focuses upon an analogous situation, in which two men are forced into an intimate relationship which both torments and satisfies them, and which simultaneously embodies certain of the tensions present in their society.

8.16   This also suggests the importance of Fugard's personal influence on the shape of the later play – underlining the need to know about him and his views. Fugard shared the prejudices of his society until at least the time he went to the 'liberal' University of Cape Town. It was a ten-month spell as the only white crew on a British tramp-steamer that, he said, cured him of racism. But it was some years later that he had that baptismal experience. He had already become actively involved in the theatre through the formation of an experimental drama group with his actress wife, when he found a temporary job as a clerk in one of the so-called 'Native Commissioner's Courts', where pass-law cases were tried. The pass that Africans were obliged by law to carry at all times (until 1986) was the keystone of white control over black South Africans. It is for burning his pass in front of a police station that Winston has ended up on 'the Island' (scene ii).

8.17   'You know, we used to send one man every two minutes to jail', Fugard later recalled, 'it was a pretty traumatic experience because finally I didn't know how to cope with that many faces going into … going nowhere …
I knew that society was evil before I had that experience, but seeing the machinery in operation taught me how it works and in fact what it does to people' (Marks, 1973). This 'traumatic experience' lies at the heart of his work, and is fundamental to what it tries to do to audiences: shock them/us into a new awareness, an awareness of what the dominant racist ideology 'does to people'. Is this enough? That depends on how you understand its ideological position – and your own.

8.18   At the same time, during the late fifties, when interracial contact was often entered into by concerned white liberals, Fugard made his first black friends in one of the ghetto 'townships'. Out of their lives he created his first full-length plays, written for and performed by black, largely amateur casts operating under rough, workshop conditions. Thereafter his plays have often drawn upon the experiences of the performers themselves. Fugard conceived *The Blood Knot*, for example, as 'inseparable' from a black jazz musician who had acted in the earlier plays, and with whom he went on to tour the country – often breaking the law in order to do so. The last (140th) production of this tour took place in New Brighton, Port Elizabeth, in March 1962. One result was that, a year later, the playwright was approached by a group of men and women from New Brighton with a request to help with their amateur drama group. This was the beginning of Serpent Players, and Fugard's association with the black actors who helped create *The Island*.

8.19   From Fugard's point of view, the group from New Brighton came with the 'old, old request', as he confided to his notebooks, 'actually it is hunger. A desperate hunger for meaningful activity – to do something that would make the hell of their daily existence meaningful' (Benson, 1983, p.81). And from the Players' point of view? This is disputed ground: unpublished letters reveal the enthusiasm and gratitude of the original members towards Fugard, the man they called their 'master spirit' and mentor, without whom, they say, nothing would have happened; subsequently the two most outstanding (and later) members, Kani and Ntshona, insisted that the initiative and the creativity came from their side and Kani gives another version in TV6.

8.20   Whatever the truth of the matter (if there is such a 'truth' to be found), it is clear that the Players began at a time when multiracial activity was still possible, despite the post-Sharpeville (i.e. post-1960) wave of repression which was eventually to destroy them; and that by the 1970s, when the three remaining collaborators, Fugard, Kani and Ntshona, had produced their major joint work in *Sizwe Bansi* and *The Island*, the emergent Black Consciousness movement (exemplified by Steve Biko) was proclaiming black people's creativity and strength while simultaneously marginalizing the contribution of whites, including 'white liberals' such as Fugard, to their struggle. Fugard's contribution to the 'struggle' may well have been marginal; but it has not been marginal to the development of black South African theatre, as black South African writers and dramatists have more recently confirmed.

8.21   But why should a group of black people – including two schoolteachers (named as 'Georgie' and 'Mulligan' in *The Island*), a lawyer's clerk, a factory worker, a bus driver and domestic servants from one of South Africa's segregated 'townships', put on plays and ask for help from a man such as Fugard? According to unpublished letters they wanted above all to 'tell their story, the story of their lives', which, they felt, had not been told before. Whatever his motives, Fugard was the first white to have written plays by, for and with black people. Furthermore, he lived not far from New Brighton. But was there no black theatre available?

8.22   In earlier, traditional African society, drama in the form of story-telling, dance and ritual had always played a vital part in the life of the community. Such traditional forms had, however, long been disrupted by the dominant European culture, with the result that the first full-length plays by Africans tended to be derivative, while the non-élite productions generally consisted of 'a series of standard scenes' renewed and enlivened by improvisation (Coplan, 1985, p.125). In the early sixties, 'black theatre' had come to mean the glossy, packaged 'shows' of so-called tribal dancing staged by white managements for white audiences, which sometimes found their way abroad where they presented an 'acceptable' (to the authorities) image of happy, bare-breasted blacks – for example, in the successful 'black musical' *Ipi Tombi* (incorrect Zulu for 'Where Are the Girls?'), which ran in London's West End shortly after *The Island*'s much more limited, 'fringe' success.

8.23   During the late seventies and early eighties an alternative, explicitly political theatre by black South Africans (such as Maishe Maponya, Zakes Mda and Percy Mtwa) developed, relying heavily upon traditional story-telling and improvisational techniques, and having a considerable impact at home and abroad. And this happened despite the absence of black professional theatres and drama schools in the country – not to mention the censorship, bannings and other restrictions imposed on playwrights and performers by the apartheid system. Although Fugard once had his passport removed (after *The Blood Knot* appeared on BBC TV), it was returned after four years and, despite harassment, his position as a white liberal playwright of international renown ensured his safety, if not always that of his actors. Thus, almost invariably, the black or multiracial groups that have survived have had sympathetic, 'liberal' whites involved in production and administration: they can obtain the money, the permits, and access to non-segregated facilities in South Africa and abroad – a pattern that preceded Fugard's involvement with the Serpent Players, but which their success helped make predominant. This pattern has also created guilt, resentment and even bitterness on both sides of the apartheid-created boundaries. It is only gradually being eroded.

8.24   Improvisation was the key to the Serpent Players' practice, and they went on to produce cheaply-mounted versions of *Woyzeck*, *The Caucasian Chalk Circle* and *Antigone*, in 'township' venues (such as St Stephen's Hall, New Brighton), without proper seating, lighting, props or backstage facilities. The Players, their relatives and friends, including the Fugards, came under surveillance from the start; but when, in 1965, a massive purge of the Eastern Cape (long a centre of militant opposition towards white rule) took place, the impact upon them was immediate: several members were arrested for allegedly belonging to the African National Congress – including the actor (Norman Ntshinga) who was about to play Haemon in *Antigone*, and who was eventually sentenced to incarceration on Robben Island. This was in June 1965, the date mentioned in scene i.

*8.25*   But the Players did not collapse. Instead, with courage and dedication, they began a new phase of 'play-making', without identifiable texts or authors, using the performers' own names and experiences, mediated by a Brechtian actor-presenter who encouraged audiences to think about, and not merely sympathize with, what they were watching. This new phase was aided by the arrival of John Kani, who replaced the arrested Ntshinga in *Antigone* in 1965, and Winston Ntshona, an old schoolfriend of Kani's from New Brighton, whom he introduced to the group two years later. Both in their mid-twenties, Kani, a janitor in the Ford plant, and Ntshona, a factory laboratory assistant, decided by 1972 to become full-time professional actors, a job category not recognized by the authorities – for whom, according to their passbooks, they were Fugard's 'servants'. Within months this joint commitment had issued in the collaborative workshop productions *Sizwe Bansi is Dead* and *The Island*.

*8.26*   According to John Kani, Fugard and the two actors had been looking for a 'two-hander' to do, preferably drawn from everyday black experience, and after toying with Soyinka's radio play *The Detainee* (1965), found the 'mandate' (Fugard's term) they needed in a photograph of a smiling black man whom, they decided, would only smile if his passbook was in order. Thus began the experiments that led to *Sizwe Bansi is Dead,* in which the central character (played by Ntshona) takes on the identity of a dead man so as to stay on and work in Port Elizabeth without harassment – although not for ever: 'A black man stay out of trouble? Impossible', as he tells his friend 'Buntu' (Kani), 'Our skin is trouble'.

*8.27*   Acting as a means of survival was central to the brilliant combination of mime, monologue, improvised dialogue and remembered gesture which ensured immediate local success, as well as the Royal Court invitation, before any written script was available. And while the group waited for permission to leave for London, they decided to apply similar workshop techniques to some of the material gleaned from friends and former colleagues on Robben Island – including a two-man version of *Antigone* arranged by Ntshinga on the basis of his memory of the play he was to perform in when arrested. After just two weeks of intensive work within view of the off-shore island itself, a play emerged called *Die Hodoshe Span*, 'Hodoshe Span', or 'Hodoshe's work-team', so named after a Robben Island warder called 'Hodoshe' (Xhosa for 'carrion-fly'). This was a usefully obscure title for the brief, 'private' local opening run, designed not to attract attention to the fact that here was a play informing its audience about matters it was strictly illegal to publish – one further reason for not having a written script.

*8.28*   Thus, it is the history of the play as an event that suggests how it might be viewed as more than simply an attack upon the ideology of apartheid, but as the incorporation of the black experience in South Africa by a 'white liberal'. But, then, we must ask when we view it now: *how far* does it oppose the explicit ideology, and how far, perhaps, does it *take it for granted*? Another way of putting this would be to ask: how far is *The Island* a tragedy with the 'universal', even 'metaphysical' implications of its central theme – the individual pitted against an overwhelming fate – and how far is it a political play, radically opposed to the society in which it was generated in that it showed the human dignity of those condemned by apartheid? If the answer seems to be both, this may well be because *The Island* reveals contradictory ideological impulses, seeming to undermine the status quo on the one hand, and yet to confirm it on the other. And are there *other* ideological dimensions to it? What gaps and silences can we see in it now?

## *The Island* as 'ideological statement'

*8.29*   *The Island* does not call for revolution. But the central character, Winston, endures everything, in defiance of the law. For how long, we do not know; the possibility is raised that he will end up like 'old Harry', who 'loves stone', who has 'forgotten everything ... why he's here, where he comes from' (scene iii). Fugard, it seems, could go no further than this; and it is unlikely that he would have become this explicit without the pressure, the demand, of his black co-creators. *The Island*'s immediate successor, *Statements After An Arrest Under the Immorality Act*, despite its title and ostensible theme, is more inward and much more characteristic of Fugard, exploring the instinctual drives that enable people to survive, despite the worst that happens to them, rather than the laws that, as Brecht said, 'man has made, and therefore can unmake!'.

*8.30*   None of those *directly* involved in the creation of *The Island* had (or have) been politically active. Yet Fugard's 'liberal' awareness of the wrongs inflicted upon his black countrymen, and Kani and Ntshona's less easily defined, but inevitably more immediate, sense of their own people's position (Kani's brother was on Robben Island at the time of the playmaking) may be said to have produced a work that spoke for them all. But did it? And does it now? It is Kani and Ntshona, not Fugard, who later asked audiences to 'endorse' it as a call for the release of South Africa's most famous political prisoner.

*8.31*   This clarifies the extent to which what the play 'means', and hence its ideology, is part of an historical process, and shifting perceptions of the issue of South Africa and apartheid – perceptions themselves bound up with your own position towards racism, and the politics of race, abroad and at home. I can't tell you what your views are, or should be, about this; they will in any case depend on your position within this changing history. What I can do is try to indicate what I see the play offering now. Let's look at the closing scene, the main 'play-within-the-play'.

## ACTIVITY

What would you say is the central point of the last scene? What ideological position can you discern in it, now that you know more about the conditions of production? It may be helpful if you focus upon the words Winston/Antigone is given, borrowed from Sophocles, at the point where he tells Creon, the king and self-styled law-giver: 'You are only a man, Creon. Even as there are laws made by men, so too there are others that come from God.'

## DISCUSSION

This touches on a number of issues central to the whole play, one of which we can sum up as follows: is this an endorsement of the call for Mandela's release? Or is it an expression of the age-old and familiar conflict between morality and the law that has ensured the durability of Sophocles' play? In other words, does this have an immediately local and specific political thrust, or a 'universal', even 'metaphysical' meaning? Or does it – can it – have both? As I have tried to suggest, our 'literary text' potentially has different meanings; what it means at any one moment depends upon the specifics of that moment: the theatre, the audience, the time and place. Considering its 'production', we should at least agree that we cannot be innocent consumers, any more than its co-creators were innocent 'producers'.

And so I have to offer the ideological position I now discern in that last scene, just as you will have to. First, consider what happens. The cell area has been transformed into a 'stage' for the prison concert, and John addresses the imaginary prison audience, including the warders and other prisoners, with a summary of the events leading to Antigone's trial. Antigone (here and in Sophocles) has defied the law and buried her brother, who had returned from exile to destroy the state (as numbers of black South African guerrillas have done). She was caught and arrested. Then begins the two-man version of the

Greek play, with John reappearing as the king to make a lengthy address in which Creon argues that he embodies the law that protects the people, but that also strikes the 'subversive elements' still 'at large'.

When the accused comes in, we might laugh (Winston is wearing a wig, necklace of nails, false breasts and a blanket for a skirt) – a response anticipated in scene ii, when we first see him like that, and then are made to realize that the point is gained if the prison audience, and ourselves, 'listen at the end'. The earlier moment, in other words, defuses as it anticipates, any possibility that the audience may find his change of role ridiculous. This has a peculiar resonance here I feel – on one level, suggesting imprisonment and emasculation, a loss of power and identity which can be temporarily overcome by acting; on another, suggesting by its very absence, the potency of the female in this prison world dominated by a masculine mode of comradeship. The original heroine was a formidable creature, uncompromising to the end: could it be that we discern through this gap, this unconsciousness in the play as we have it, an accommodation with the patriarchy of Creon – the Greek Antigone's uncle, and by no means a tyrant to begin with? But I leave the possibilities for you to explore further. In the Fugard/Kani/Ntshona play's conclusion, what we have on the simplest, strongest level is Winston as Antigone, pleading guilty according to the law made by the state embodied in Creon; he also asks if Creon is God, before accepting the punishment laid down. Then Winston tears off his costume and confronts the audience as himself. The play-within-the-play is concluded, the Greek tragedy reactivated, in order to show us a hero: the black man going to his 'living death', unrepentant. In the original *Antigone* the protagonist has killed herself by the end of the play, and so no longer poses any threat to Creon or the laws of the state. But *this* version ends *before* the 'tragic' development of the original, and the cathartic resolution of its basic underlying conflict. Moreover, *we* are left with that concluding image of the two men shackled together again, running, as the siren wails and darkness descends.

It seems to me that what we have here is, on the one hand, an emphasis upon individual morality as opposed to law and the state. This is a 'liberal' position. But there is also, on the other hand, an emphasis upon black brotherhood – most obvious in the reference to 'Son of the Land', the third time this phrase has been used (initially in the form *Nyana we Sizwe*). Which emphasis is overriding? That depends for me upon the emphasis of performance, which will depend upon the circumstances, the 'production' in the sense I have been using. Being shackled together is hardly 'brotherhood' but it may allow for, indeed encourage, a recognition of brotherhood, of human strength through suffering imposed by a common foe. I find myself unable to forget the two men helping each other at the beginning, tending each other's wounds, when I see them running again at the end. For me, then, the words (whether from Antigone, as most of those in the last scene are, or from the improvised debates conducted by Fugard, Kani and Ntshona in Cape Town in the early 1970s) ultimately matter less for the play's lasting impact than the physical presences, the dramatic image.

This suggests the unique strength of the play as we can now come to it, or 'read' it: it can be understood as offering a spectrum – but within certain crucial limits – of possibilities. At one limit, the least it does is 'state' the horror, the 'living death' to which countless people have been, and are being, condemned for their opposition to an abhorrent and indefensible system of beliefs. At the other, the most it has to offer is an awareness that what seems to be given, or natural, or the way things are, enshrined by law and 'common sense', is actually constructed, 'made by men' – in short, it is an ideology. The play is, if you like, *about* ideology. It is, in Adorno's terms, a successful example of a 'committed' work of art: i.e. 'not intended to generate ameliorative measures, legislative acts or practical institutions … but to work at the level of fundamental attitudes' (Reader, p.91). The possibility of a continuing provocation is made obvious if we recall how the play originally emerged. It is also, to my mind, the only useful way in which it can be said to have a 'universal' or, as I would prefer to use that term, a cross-cultural theme, one that we can apply to ourselves within our own cultures.

# 9  Adorno: Commitment and the autonomy of literature

9.1  You have twice already considered some aspects of Theodor Adorno's essay on *Commitment*: in relation to 'A Sahibs' War' and *The Island*. Now I want to return to the opening and middle parts of it again, though not for the last time. Much of the essay is concerned with Brecht, whose *Mother Courage* is a text for Block 8, but Adorno also refers to Beckett, so we can refer back to *Endgame*, which will enable you to draw together some general aspects of your work on drama so far. And the issues debated here will also be relevant to your next play, *Sergeant Musgrave's Dance* in Block 5. But although most of Adorno's major examples are from drama, what he has to say is just as relevant to other literary forms.

9.2  The essay is challenging, and refers to authors and texts that we cannot expect you to know. This is true, of course, of many of the Reader texts – they were not written with this course in mind. But learning to be at ease with critical and theoretical disquisitions that refer to more than you know is one of the skills we want you to acquire, and I doubt whether every member of the course team is familiar with every learned reference! Besides, Adorno seems to me specially worth the struggle, whether one agrees with his political position or not. He is passionately convinced that literature matters, and expresses himself (often with mordant humour) in terms that demand a response. As we have stressed with all the other writers in this block, it is specially important to be aware of the circumstances in which he was writing. He was a German Marxist who spent the Nazi years exiled in the USA. When he wrote this, the Berlin Wall had just been completed.

## ACTIVITY

Will you now read the first paragraphs down to '… as they have always been' (pp.89–95).

9.3  The contest between 'committed and autonomous literature' takes us back to Block 2, and whether art should have a 'message' or stand aloof and 'autonomous'. We also referred briefly to 'relative autonomy' in the first section of this block: that is, the notion that whereas works of art are inevitably the product of their times, they may also be partly produced by the artistic traditions of which they form a part, and so be *relatively* free of economic determination. Then at the end of the *Yerma* case-study, we referred you to Sartre, whose ideas Adorno is here challenging. Sartre, you'll remember, saw commitment as imperative: history, he claimed, made it morally unthinkable for the writer to remain aloof. But Adorno insists that the 'Sartrean goats and the Valeryan sheep will not be separated'. (The French symbolist poet Paul Valéry exemplified the 'art for art's sake' position.) You have already considered this when debating how far the Modernist manifesto on this issue was practicable: see Block 2 Section 9. Where Adorno differs most from Sartre is in his insistence that the significance of a work of literature does not reside in its 'meanings' alone, but in those autonomous aspects of it that we might for simplicity's sake think of as its 'art'.

9.4    The following paragraph from Adorno's essay, which is not given in the Reader, takes us back to *Yerma* and the outcry in the right-wing press that greeted its first performance:

> Newspapers and magazines of the radical Right constantly stir up
> indignation against what is unnatural, over-intellectual, morbid and
> decadent: they know their readers. The insights of social psychology into the
> authoritarian personality confirm them. The basic features of this type
> include conformism, respect for a petrified façade of opinion and society,
> and resistance to impulses that disturb its order or evoke inner elements of
> the unconscious that cannot be admitted. This hostility to anything alien or
> alienating can accommodate itself much more easily to literary realism of
> any provenance, even if it proclaims itself critical or socialist, than to works
> which swear allegiance to no political slogans, but whose mere guise is
> enough to disrupt the whole system of rigid coordinates that governs
> authoritarian personalities – to which the latter cling all the more fiercely,
> the less capable they are of spontaneous appreciation of anything not
> officially approved … when the social contract with reality is abandoned,
> and literary works no longer speak as though they were reporting fact, hairs
> start to bristle. Not the least of the weaknesses of the debate on commitment
> is that it ignores the effect produced by works whose own formal laws pay
> no heed to coherent effects. So long as it fails to understand what the shock
> of the unintelligible can communicate, the whole dispute resembles
> shadow-boxing.

9.5    *Yerma* is not overtly political in the way that *The Island* unmistakably is, nor could it have been attacked as 'over-intellectual'. But its critics might well have denounced it as 'morbid' – possessed with a dangerous tendency to make people (especially women) dissatisfied with their lot. The derision that met early productions of Beckett in this country, and many of the British plays written in the late 50s and 60s (as you'll see in Block 5), was frequently couched in the very terms Adorno identifies. *Yerma* 'evoke[s] inner elements of the unconscious that cannot be admitted' by the Right because they disturb the 'petrified façade'. *Look Back in Anger* and *Serjeant Musgrave's Dance* were to have a similar effect. But these latter works, like *The Island*, are overtly defiant. Where Adorno advances Sartre's arguments is that he includes work whose power lies – like Beckett's – in 'the shock of the unintelligible'.

9.6    In the paragraphs that follow (which are in the Reader), Adorno refers to both Sartre's and Brecht's plays, but you don't need to know them to be able to follow the gist of what he is saying: that the formal demands of art (the need to invent plots and representative characters for example) tend to confuse or subvert the very ideas that it was their author's intention to express. The work we have done on post-Althusserian ideas of ideology may help us out of this impasse. In *The Island*, for example, the prisoners chose to put on a version of Sophocles' *Antigone*. You might think that by selecting a play that is part of the dominant (white) culture, the play's African claims have been weakened. But if, instead of thinking of the authors' commitment in a narrow, overt sense, we think of the unconscious, 'lived' operations of ideology, I think we can see in the play a call on a *shared* image of oppression, which may or may not universalize the experience (as Dennis Walder suggests), but which certainly reproduces some of the ideological entanglements that are a feature of life under apartheid. Althusser allows us to get beyond the idea of commitment as a Sartrean *choice*. Lorca's overt commitment was less specific. It was partly the very absence of much reference to traditional religious forms and values that signalled his opposition to the Nationalist programme. Yet the forms of his drama – his use of folk-motifs for example – also signal a radical conservatism. But the absence of an overt political platform in any narrow sense was not evasive – as the extreme reaction to his work decisively proved.

9.7   We shall postpone a full discussion of Adorno's critique of Brecht until Block 8, but some of his more generally applicable arguments can be debated here. He distinguishes between Brecht, who committed his art to the exposition of a precise political programme, and Sartre, who posits his ideas of commitment on *choice*. Perhaps in this block the example that most clearly takes as 'its task ... to awaken the free choice of the agent' (the phrase occurs in the paragraph beginning 'In aesthetic theory...', pp.90–91) is Camus's *The Outsider*, where the reader is allowed what you may have found a disconcerting freedom. In Sartre, Adorno exposes a gap between theory and artistic practice, because his plays tend to suggest that freedom is illusory. This you are not in a position to judge, but the same paragraph contains some bracingly prescriptive pronouncements: would you agree, for example, that '*It is not the office of art to spotlight alternatives, but to resist by its form alone the course of the world*'? Whether or not that is art's *office*, it certainly seems to be its practice. Resistance, either particularized or generalized, seems to be the driving force of both the plays we have just studied. Sheer contrariness sometimes seems to me to be Kipling's political baseline. Spark perhaps exploits the Sartrean position to the full by suggesting that there may be radiant virtues even in someone as woefully wrong as Miss Brodie. Camus's Meursault is as indifferent to the rights of the world as its wrongs, and O'Connor suggests that the course of the world is out of our hands altogether. As Adorno concludes, 'commitment thus slides towards the proclivities of the author'. It seems that though we might like to be rid of the author, there must remain a sense in which every work of art is fundamentally subjective.

9.8   In the paragraph beginning 'Sartre will not allow...' Adorno begins to develop an argument for a partial autonomy of artistic form: '*every work of art ... confronts the writer, however free he may be, with objective demands of composition*', and '*the author's motivations are irrelevant to the finished work*'. I expect you will have heard writers declare, when describing the processes of composition, that a novel or a poem or a play has 'a life of its own', which 'takes over'. It is not enough to want to write about apartheid, or Fascism, or the grace of God: if you are not writing an essay, you have to find an expressive form – a plot, characters, revealing incidents. Adorno goes on to exemplify this at a much more sophisticated level in the paragraph beginning: '...however sublime' (p.92). Here he suggests that commitment does not necessarily reside in the abstract ideas, but among what he memorably calls the 'race of aesthetic forms'.

9.9   Brecht tried to solve this – as we shall see – by inventing new theatrical forms, and attempting to get away from psychologically realistic and individualized characterization: 'The People on his stage shrink before our eyes into the agents of social processes and functions.' But – again, as we shall see – even his art rose up against his intentions.

9.10   We can pass over the paragraphs that deal with the developments in Brecht's work for now, but the end of the long paragraph beginning 'Contemporary literary Germany' (pp.94–5) concludes with some challenging generalizations. Consider the following:

> ...the less works have to proclaim what they cannot completely believe themselves, the more telling they become in their own right; and the less they need a surplus of meaning beyond what they are.

In a memorable sentence, which the pressures of space have excluded from the Reader extracts, Adorno says that when Brecht became a 'panegyrist' of 'coercive domination', 'his lyric voice had to swallow chalk, and it started to grate'. This harsh, unhealthy friction, produced when political ideas are not lubricated by the conflicting demands of art, does not seem to me to be a feature of any of our chosen texts. In discussing *The Island*, you were asked to consider whether the play is a narrowly ideological work, *only* an anti-apartheid play. Dennis Walder argued that your response to it would depend upon your stance on apartheid, although he also quotes a critical opinion that sees Fugard's plays as universalizing the local issues they deal with: 'The problems', the critic writes, 'are ultimately metaphysical'. Adorno, too, seems to open the dangerous, alluring metaphysical ground once again. *The Island* hits us very hard, and not (I think) just because someone like me (a white, liberal humanist) is economically enmeshed in South African politics, whether I want it or not, but because it simultaneously addresses a precise political injustice, and transcends it. *The Island* will not become a mere historical curiosity even if the political circumstances that produced it are eradicated, just as *Yerma* has not, despite more than a decade of democracy in Spain. The Algerian War is all but forgotten outside Algeria and France, yet *The Outsider* still speaks to us; and it is not just because Britain still has some remnants of Empire that we can read 'A Sahibs' War' with profit. What Adorno's writing exposes is that vestiges of the essentialist, transcendent case (so often asserted, so seldom effectively theorized) remain – and that art transforms (even transfigures) politics.

*9.11*   This does *not* give us permission to waffle on endlessly about the mysteries of art instead of trying to understand how it functions. Throughout this block we have tried to unravel something of the complex relationship between ideas and the expression of them in a variety of literary and dramatic forms. What it does reveal is how inconclusive in some vital respects our search has been. But should we expect it to be otherwise? We began this block by looking at some relatively unsophisticated tenets of Marxist theory, which may have seemed to promise a scientific approach to literature – as if, once the theory had been sufficiently refined, it could be applied and would produce an answer. Then, in all the case-studies, we confronted the persistently elusive nature of each complex instance. In the terms of Adorno's dichotomy, we identified those aspects of each work that were autonomous – of art – rather than straightforwardly committed, and we found that those aspects (which were frequently absences as much as presences) modified the commitment.

*9.12*   There are claims in the remainder of the essay that are, again, more germane to the themes of Block 8, *Literature and History*, and there is no space to discuss them here. But read through to the end if you have time now. Many of the issues that have been raised here will not receive as much attention in the intervening blocks, which have their own themes to pursue. But that does not – of course – mean that you cannot apply the ways of thinking you have practised here to what is to come. All of the texts in Block 5 will be enriched if you search in them for evidence of 'lived' ideology, for significant silences, and for how each work's particular commitment is modified by the autonomy of its art.

# 10 References

ABERCROMBIE, N. (1984) *The Penguin Dictionary of Sociology*, Penguin Books.

ALTHER, L. (ed.) (1980) *A Good Man is Hard to Find*, The Women's Press.

ALTHUSSER, L. (1983) 'Ideology and ideological state apparatuses' in *Essays on Ideology*, Verso.

ANDERSON, R. (1984) *Federico García Lorca*, Macmillan.

ARENDT, H. (1958) *The Origins of Totalitarianism*, Meridian Books.

BENSON, M. (ed.) (1983) *Athol Fugard: Notebooks 1960–1977*, Faber.

BLINKHORN, M. (1988) *Democracy and Civil War in Spain 1931–1939*, Routledge.

BOLD, A. (ed.) (1984) *An Odd Capacity for Vision*, Vision Press and Barnes and Noble.

BRUCE, S. (1985) *No Pope of Rome*, Mainstream (Edinburgh).

CAIRNS CRAIG, R. (ed.) (1988) *History of Scottish Literature*, Vol. 4, Aberdeen University Press.

CALVIN, J. (1961) *Concerning the Eternal Predestination of God*, Clarke (Cambridge).

CAMUS, A. (1975) *The Myth of Sisyphus* (trans. J. O'Brien), Penguin Books.

CARR, R. (1989) *Spain 1875–1980*, Oxford Paperbacks.

CARRINGTON, C. (1955) *Rudyard Kipling – His Life and Work*, Macmillan.

COLES, R. (1980) *Flannery O'Connor's South*, Louisiana State University Press.

COPLAN, D. (1985) *In Township Tonight: South Africa's black city music and theatre*, Longman.

EAGLETON, T. (1976) *Marxism and Literary Criticism*, Methuen.

ENSOR, R.C.K. (1936) *The Oxford History of England*, Vol. XIV, Oxford University Press.

FITZGERALD, R. (1965), introduction to *Everything that Rises Must Converge*, Farrar, Straus and Giroux.

FITZGERALD, R. and FITZGERALD, S. (eds) (1972) *Mystery and Manners: the occasional prose of Flannery O'Connor*, Faber.

FUGARD, A. (1987) *Selected Plays*, Oxford University Press.

FUGARD, A., KANI, J., NTSHONA, W. (1974) *Selected Plays*, Oxford University Press.

GIBSON, I. (1989) *Federico García Lorca*, Faber.

GIBSON, I. (1983) *The Assassination of Federico García Lorca*, Penguin.

GORDIMER, N. (1976) 'English – language, literature and politics' in HEYWOOD, C (ed.) *Aspects of South African Literature*, Heinemann.

GRAMSCI, A. (1971) *Selections from the Prison Notebooks*, Lawrence and Wishart.

GRASS, G. (1987) *On Writing and Politics*, Penguin.

HEYWOOD, C. (ed.) (1976) *Aspects of South African Literature*, Heineman.

KERSHAW, I. (1987) *The Hitler Myth*, Oxford University Press.

LODGE, D. (1971) *The Novelist at the Crossroads and other essays*, Routledge and Kegan Paul.

LYON, J. (1987) 'General Introduction' to *Yerma*, Aris and Philips.

McCARTHY, P. (1988) *Albert Camus: The Stranger*, Cambridge University Press.

McDERMOTT, P. (1988) 'Lorca: Crisis and Commitment', in *Leeds Papers*.

MACHEREY, P. (1978) 'Lenin, critic of Tolstoy' in *A Theory of Literary Production* (trans. G. Wall), Routledge and Kegan Paul.

MacPHERSON, P. and MINETT, P. (1987), introduction and notes to LORCA, F.G. *Yerma*, Aris and Phillips.

MARKS, J. (1973) 'Interview with Athol Fugard', *Yale/Theatre*, iv (1), pp.64–72

MARWICK, A. (1980) *Class: image and reality*, Collins.

MASSIE, A. (1979) *Muriel Spark*, Ramsay Head (Edinburgh).

MASTERS, B. (1974) *A Student's Guide to Camus*, Fontana.

MILLAR, K. (ed.) (1970) *Memoirs Of A Modern Scotland*, Faber.

NIVEN, A. (1975) 'Athol Fugard in Britain', *Commonwealth Newsletter*, no. 7.

O'CONNOR, F. (1972) *Mystery and Manners*, Faber.

O'CONNOR, F. (1979) *The Habit of Being*, Farrar, Straus and Giroux.

THE OPEN UNIVERSITY (1986) A102 An Arts Foundation Course, Units 20–2 *Moral values and the social order* and Units 22–6 *Culture: production, consumption and status*, The Open University.

REITZ, D. (1929) *Commando*, Faber.

RHODES, A. (1987) *Propaganda*, Wellfleet Press.

ROSS, M.C. (1963) 'Flannery O'Connor: an interview', *Jubilee*, XI, June.

VANDENBROUCKE, R. (1985) *Truths the Hand Can Touch,* Theatre Communications Group.

WALDER, D. (1984) *Athol Fugard*, Macmillan.

WELLS, J. (1962) 'Off the Cuff', *Critic*, Aug–Sep.

WHITTAKER, R.R. (1982) *The Faith and Fiction of Muriel Spark*, Macmillan.

WILLIAMS, R. (1983) *Keywords: a vocabulary of culture and society*, Fontana.

## Acknowledgements

Grateful acknowledgement is given to the following sources for permission to reproduce material in this block; Camus, A. *The Outsider* (trans. by Laredo, J.) Hamish Hamilton/Alfred A. Knopf, 1983; Camus, A. *The Myth of Sisyphus* (trans. by O'Brien, J.) Hamish Hamilton/Alfred A. Knopf, 1955.

Cover illustration: John Hassall (1868–1948) *Gunfight*; Collection of Simon Houfe. Photograph reproduced from Simon Houfe *The Dictionary of British Book Illustrators 1800–1914* (1977) Woodbridge, Antique Collectors Club Ltd by permission of the publisher and owner.